from Arthur

12/98

The Complete Poems
of Stephen Crane

The Complete Poems of
STEPHEN CRANE

Edited with an Introduction by

JOSEPH KATZ

Cornell Paperbacks

Cornell University Press

Ithaca and London

 The poems are reprinted from *The Poems of Stephen Crane: A Special Edition,* Second Printing—Revised, by special arrangement with Cooper Square Publishers, Incorporated, 59 Fourth Avenue, New York, New York 10003.

First published 1972 by Cornell University Press.
First printing, Cornell Paperbacks, 1972.

Printed in the United States of America.

Library of Congress Cataloging in Publication Data
(For library cataloging purposes only)

Crane, Stephen, 1871–1900.
The complete poems of Stephen Crane.

(Cornell Paperbacks)
Includes bibliographical references.
I. Katz, Joseph, ed. II. Title.
[PS1449.C85A17 1972] 811'.4 76-38682
ISBN 0-8014-9130-4 (pbk. : alk. paper)

Cornell University Press strives to utilize environmentally responsible suppliers and materials to the fullest extent possible in the publishing of its books. Such materials include vegetable-based, low-VOC inks and acid-free papers that are also either recycled, totally chlorine-free, or partly composed of nonwood fibers.

Paperback printing 10 9

FOR EDWIN H. CADY

AND HORST FRENZ

Contents

Preface

This book contains every poem known to have been written by Crane. They are reprinted here from *The Poems of Stephen Crane: A Critical Edition,* Second Printing—Revised (New York: Cooper Square Publishers, 1971). That is a scholarly edition. It contains a detailed statement of the textual theory from which the poems were edited, a record of all editorial emendations, the textual history of each poem, and so on. The aim of this edition is to make the established texts available for the widest possible use, so the scholarly apparatus has been omitted. The introduction here is a revised version of the one in the earlier edition.

JOSEPH KATZ

Columbia, South Carolina

Acknowledgments

Two important debts are recorded on another page. I owe additional thanks to Edwin H. Cady for stimulating this work and for commenting on the stages through which it progressed. James K. Hastie patiently listened to my flights of theory and read through many manuscripts, Vincent Starrett commented on an early version, and Fredson Bowers on the editorial principles.

Librarians and libraries of considerable assistance to me were David A. Randall, Miss Geneva Warner, Mrs. Doris M. Read, and William Cagle of the Lilly and University Libraries of Indiana University; the late Roland Baughman and Kenneth A. Lohf of the Butler Library of Columbia University; William H. Runge, Miss Anne Freudenberg, and Miss Elizabeth Ryall of the Alderman Library of the University of Virginia; John S. Mayfield and Lester G. Wells, both formerly of the Syracuse University Library; Miss Anna Brooke Allan and James W. Patton of the University of North Carolina Library; the late John D. Gordan of the Berg Collection of the New York Public Library. I offer additional thanks to these institutions for permission to publish material of which they are the possessors.

I owe further debts to Clifton Waller Barrett; to Robert W. Stallman; to Owen Thomas; to William A. Koshland of Alfred A. Knopf Incorporated; to Gay Wilson Allen; to David H. Dickason; to Maurice Bassan; to Pierre Baillet; to Matthew J. Bruccoli; to Daniel G. Hoffman; and to Henry Chafetz and Sidney B. Solomon of Cooper Square Publishers.

For permission to publish from the manuscripts and letters of Stephen Crane, and for permission to reprint from

The Work of Stephen Crane and *The Collected Poems,* I thank Alfred A. Knopf Incorporated, owners of the literary rights to Crane's writings.

Finally, I thank Karen for the intelligence, the understanding, and the fairly consistent good humor with which she has borne her trials.

Introduction

"Personally, I like my little book of poems, 'The Black Riders,' better than I do 'The Red Badge of Courage,' " Stephen Crane said in mid-career. "The reason is, I suppose, that the former is the more serious effort. In it I aim to give my ideas of life as a whole, so far as I know it, and the latter is a mere episode—an amplification." [1] He was playing that game of indirection in which a writer tries to interest those who are curious about one book in reading another, but he was making a serious point too. Crane's first volume of poetry was an expression of his world view both more comprehensive and more compact than anything else he had written up to that time. Four years later his second and last book of poems, *War Is Kind,* confirmed and deepened the insights of the other book. Crane was right: his poetry reveals the pattern of thought that lies behind all his writings. His is a vision of the world in which the gods have departed and man is left alone to fend for himself.

No one knows when he began writing poetry. But in the summer of 1891 he met Hamlin Garland, who was on the Jersey shore, giving a series of lectures on the topic of "American Literature and Expressive Art." Crane was work-

[1] Crane to *DeMorest's Family Magazine,* XXXII (May 1896), 399–400; in Joseph Katz, ed., *The Portable Stephen Crane* (New York, 1969), pp. 534–35. That letter seems to derive from a formal response he drafted in answer to a large number of requests for information about the author of *The Red Badge of Courage*. Other descendants of the form are Crane to John Northern Hilliard, January 2, 1896; in R. W. Stallman and Lillian Gilkes, eds., *Stephen Crane: Letters* (New York, 1960), pp. 93–96; a letter quoted in J. Herbert Welch, "The Personality and Work of Stephen Crane," *Leslie's Weekly,* May 28, 1896 (*Letters,* pp. 78–79); and a letter quoted in Hilliard, "Stephen Crane: Letters to a Friend About His Ambition, His Art, and His Views of Life," New York *Times,* July 14, 1900, p. 466 (*Letters,* pp. 158–59).

ing for his brother's New Jersey Coast News Bureau, a small-time operation that fed news of the resorts to newspapers such as the New York *Tribune*. When that newspaper published Crane's article, "Howells Discussed at Avon-by-the-Sea," he used a clipping to introduce himself to Garland, who was pleased by Crane's accuracy and enthusiasm. The reporter, in turn, liked Garland's ideas, and his attention. He described the older writer as "like a nice Jesus Christ." [2] They talked a lot that summer, throwing a baseball back and forth, and building a pleasant, casual relationship.

They resumed the acquaintance when Garland returned the next August. This time Crane showed him a clipping of a report on an Asbury Park parade. The Junior Order of United American Mechanics had marched raggedly past a review of idling vacationers, and the tableau suggested ironies to Crane. He had written them, and had been fired. It was an election year; the publisher of the *Tribune* was running for Vice President, and his opponents were happy for an occasion to protest. Garland deplored the situation, but Crane was, after all, no more than a talented young reporter and a casual acquaintance. Whatever Crane had expected, the situation called for little more. Garland had no reason to believe that within a few years Crane would realize the literary revolution for which he and Howells had been working.

A portent of that possibility was a yellow-wrappered novel that arrived in the mail the following spring. By then Crane had drifted to New York and part-time newspaper work. One day he saw a group of slum children playing a game of King of the Mountain—but with rocks instead of snowballs. He built *Maggie: A Girl of the Streets* on the incident. In excoriating the society which encouraged ignorance and self-destruction at its bottom strata, Crane had again been indiscreet. But on the strength of *Maggie,* Garland interested William Dean Howells in him. Sometime between March 29

[2] Thomas Beer, *Stephen Crane: A Study in American Letters* (New York, 1923), p. 60.

and April 8, 1893, Howells had Crane to tea, praised him above Mark Twain, and read to him from one of the posthumously published volumes of Emily Dickinson's poetry.[3] He was taken with Crane, "struck almost as much by his presence as by his mind." [4] It was a heady experience. Crane had patrons, and shamelessly dropped the names "Howells" and "Garland" into his letters. He was on his way.

Yet it is difficult to specify the consequences of what had happened. It is traditionally supposed that the Howells tea led Crane to write poetry. That story originates in a memoir by John D. Barry, editor of *The Forum*, who liked the poems better than *Maggie*.[5] The story may be true. Quite possibly, hearing the poetry that Howells had read started Crane writing his own; but considering Crane's situation at the time, there is at least an equal chance that Howells' enthusiasm was enough by itself. Doubtless, Crane had written poetry of a sort before he composed what became *The Black Riders and Other Lines*. It is even possible that a lengendary volume of erotic verse, *Cantharides*, preceded it.[6] But Corwin Knapp Linson, who knew Crane in New York, says that "Ah, haggard purse, why ope thy mouth" (*118*), was written in December 1892, and this verse, while in the line of Chaucer's lament to his purse, is no more than doodling.[7]

[3] Howells could have read from either *Poems by Emily Dickinson* (1890) or *Poems by Emily Dickinson: Second Series* (1891). The third series was not published until 1896.

[4] Howells to Cora Crane, July 29, 1900; in *Letters*, p. 306.

[5] Barry, "A Note on Stephen Crane," *Bookman*, XIII (April 1901), 148. Crane had sent Barry *Maggie* soon after it was published, and Barry replied with a detailed criticism that ended with an invitation for Crane to call on him. See Barry to Crane, March 22, 1893; Katz, "John Daniel Barry to Stephen Crane: A New Letter," *Stephen Crane Newsletter*, II (Fall 1967), 1–3.

[6] Vincent Starrett, *Stephen Crane: A Bibliography* (Philadelphia, 1923), pp. 10–11, notes: "*Cantharides*—Said to have been a collection of erotic verse, the manuscript of which was seen by several persons. Untraced."

[7] Italic numbers within parentheses identify poems in this edition. Linson, *My Stephen Crane*, Edwin H. Cady, ed. (Syracuse, New York, 1958), p. 44. See also Daniel G. Hoffman, *The Poetry of Stephen Crane* (New York, 1957), p. 181.

The poems in *The Black Riders and Other Lines* are serious work that may well have been touched off by Howells' reading of Emily Dickinson. Crane is himself no help in dating them, and Thomas Beer, his first biographer, threw up his hands and declared that "a fog rests on the birth of 'Black Riders.' " Harvey Wickham, an old schoolmate, responded, "Maybe so, but I have good reasons for thinking that this first voice of free verse was reduced to words in three days at Twin Lakes [where Crane and friends had camped during the summers of 1893 and 1894]. Crane subsequently told me that it was the outcome of a fit of desperation. 'No one would print a line of mine,' he said, 'and I just had to do something odd to attract attention.' " [8] But Wickham had not been there; he was reporting something Crane is supposed to have told him after Wickham snubbed him. Linson, who had been with Crane, in the woods and afterward, recalled that it was in mid-February 1894 that Crane first showed him his poem.[9]

Soon after, Crane left his Twenty-third Street billet for Garland's One Hundred and Fifth Street apartment to recruit his aid in placing them. He put on a performance there that probably was calculated to play on several of Garland's interests. So successful was he that Garland wrote about the scene again and again. Crane carried the manuscripts of some poems in the pocket of his ulster, waited until Garland asked him what he had, then read them to him. Garland was at first amused, and in the end struck by their power:

They were at once quaintly humorous and audacious, unrhymed and almost without rhythm, but the figures employed with masterly brevity were colossal. They suggested some of the French translations of Japanese verses, at other times they carried the sting and compression of Emily Dickinson's verse and the savage

[8] Wickham, "Stephen Crane at College," *American Mercury,* VII (March 1926), 291–97. This memoir is unreliable.

[9] Linson, *My Stephen Crane,* p. 48.

philosophy of Olive Schriner [*sic*], and yet they were not imitative.[10]

Were there more? "I have four or five up here all in a little row," replied Crane; and, without a moment's hesitation, he dashed off "God fashioned the ship of the world carefully" (*6*). Intentionally or not, he had struck precisely the attitude to capture Garland's interest.[11] A future president of the

[10] Garland's divergent accounts are: "Stephen Crane: A Soldier of Fortune," *Saturday Evening Post,* CLXXIII (July 28, 1900), 16–17, and *Book-Lover,* II (Autumn 1900), 6–7; "Stephen Crane as I Knew Him," *Yale Review,* III (April 1914), 494–506; "Roadside Meetings of a Literary Nomad," *Bookman,* LXX (January 1930), 523–28; *Roadside Meetings* (New York, 1930), pp. 189–206. Attempts to reconcile their inconsistencies include Donald Pizer's "The Garland-Crane Relationship," *Huntington Library Quarterly,* XXIV (November 1960), 75–82; Olov W. Fryckstedt, "Crane's *Black Riders:* A Discussion of Dates," *Studia Neophilologica,* XXXIV (1962), 281–93; and Stanley Wertheim, "The Saga of March 23rd: Garland, Gilder, and Crane," *Stephen Crane Newsletter,* III (Winter 1968), 1–3. Garland's vision of Crane as an automatic writer who worked under the influence of occult forces—an impression Crane did nothing to dispel—is at least in part responsible for his muddle.

The quotation is from *Roadside Meetings,* pp. 193–95. Two allusions deserve comment. One refers to "French translations of Japanese verses." A wave of interest in Japan swept over France after Perry opened the country to western trade in 1854, and this interest was revealed not only in verse but also in painting, music, and even dress. The second allusion is to Olive Schreiner (1855–1920), who was a South African writer and feminist who won popularity in the 1880s and '90s under the name "Ralph Iron." Linson (*My Stephen Crane,* p. 34) says that Crane admired her *Story of an African Farm;* so he may have read *Dreams,* a sequence of allegories. If so, that may have influenced his poetry. This possibility is explored in Carlin T. Kindilien, "Stephen Crane and the 'Savage Philosophy' of Olive Schreiner," *Boston University Studies in English,* III (Summer 1957), 97–107; and in Hoffman, *The Poetry of Stephen Crane,* pp. 195–200. A confluence, however, is more likely than an influence: Crane, the minister's son, would have had intimate contacts with the parent form of the dream-allegory Schreiner used, the parable.

[11] Garland, T. E. Allen, and B. O. Flower, "Report of Dark Sèance, with a Non-Professional Psychic, for Voices and the Movement of Objects Without Contact," *Psychical Review,* II (November 1893–February 1894), 152–77.

Garland's impression is recorded in his copy of *The Black Riders and Other Lines,* now at the Baker Library, Dartmouth College: "New York | Mar 18 | 1924 | I saw Crane set down some of these lines while sitting at my

American Psychical Association, Garland had recently come from a series of sittings with a psychic and had collaborated on an article describing the phenomena he had seen. He was always sensitive to indications of unworldly forces, so what Crane had done impressed him. Garland rushed the poems to Howells, declaring them a spiritualistic find.

Howells agreed that they were the output of a singularly creative talent, even though in elements they resembled prior work, but he had reservations. He tried to interest Henry Mills Alden in taking them for *Harper's Magazine,* but when he failed he wrote Crane, "I wish you had given them more form, for then things so striking would have found a public ready made for them; as it is they will have to make one." [12] And eight months later he confessed that he found them "too orphic," not "solid and real," and predicted the demise of the "prose poem." [13] Howells' belief that Crane's poetry lacked form and broke with tradition to the point that it did not communicate underlay his review of *The Black Riders and Other Lines* when it was published.[14] In any case, neither Howells nor Garland found a publisher for Stephen Crane's poems. That task fell to John D. Barry.

"Shortly before I left for the West," wrote Garland about Crane, "he called to tell me that he had shown his verses to Mr. John D. Barry and that Mr. Barry had 'fired them off to Copeland and Day'." [15] In a very real sense, Crane found a

desk. Evidently they were composed subconsciously and (as he said) needed only to be drawn off [by] way of his pen's point." In *Letters,* p. 334.

[12] Howells to Crane, March 18, 1894; in *Letters,* p. 31.

[13] Howells to Crane, October 2, 1894; in *Letters,* p. 40. But see Howells' introduction to Stuart Merrill's *Pastels in Prose* (New York, 1890), in which he says "it has come to stay" (p. vii).

[14] "Life and Letters," *Harper's Weekly,* XL (January 25, 1896), 79.

[15] *Roadside Meetings,* p. 200. Barry (1866–1942), had been so impressed by the poems that he read them before the Uncut Leaves Society at Sherry's restaurant on April 14, 1894. In the audience was the wife of the noted critic and poet Edmund Clarence Stedman, who later invited a contribution from Crane to his prestigious *An American Anthology* (New York, 1900). A report of the reading (reprinted in *My Stephen Crane,* pp. 55–56) appeared in the New York *Tribune* for April 16, 1894.

public "ready made" for his poetry. It was one that was built in part by the influence of William Morris over American publishing. Morris had reacted violently against the ugliness that was one result of the mechanical revolution in England, and had turned to the Middle Ages for the period of art's fullest development there.[16] The scribe had made the medieval book into a thing of beauty, to be looked at as well as into; Morris saw no reason why a mass-produced book of the eighties and nineties could not be the same. If, in designing his Kelmscott Press books, he erred perhaps too much on the side of beauty (to echo Holbrook Jackson's judgment [17])—producing books so covered with ornament and intricate black letter type that they were hard to read, books bound in vellum that snapped shut, books so heavy that a lectern was essential, and books so expensive that only the few could buy—it was no great matter; he had indicated a publishing esthetic that his followers frequently could realize.

The trend took two directions in this country, and Crane was involved in both. Such a man as Elbert Hubbard applied Morris's doctrine for shock effect, with little sensitivity producing artsy-craftsy books compounded of fine materials, indifferent workmanship, and bad taste. But men such as Herbert Copeland and Frederick Holland Day helped to stimulate the production of books that were at once experimental and tasteful:

Small and light, they are real reading volumes, favorably distinguished in their charming bindings from the drab mechanical carelessness of the ordinary editions of those years. Here, too, one finds the use of color and ornament, gold or silver stamped upon simple cloth covers, or boards completely covered with paper, gray or in colorful ornamental patterns.[18]

[16] G. D. H. Cole, ed., *William Morris: Prose, Verse, Lectures, and Essays* (London, 1948), p. 476.

[17] "The Typography of William Morris,"; in Paul A. Bennett, ed., *Books and Printing* (Cleveland and New York, 1963), pp. 233–38.

[18] Hellmut Lehmann-Haupt, *The Book in America* (New York, 1951), p. 324.

In its six years (1893–1899) the house reflected the wealth, eccentricity, and artistic staunchness of Frederick Day and the knowledgeability and restraint of Herbert Copeland. Of the ninety-six titles in the Copeland & Day catalogue, fifty-four were books of poetry. The inclusion of Stephen Crane's *The Black Riders and Other Lines* among these can be set down in part to the friendship between Copeland and John D. Barry during their undergraduate days at Harvard, at a time when that institution was turning out many of the leaders of the experimental movement in publishing.[19]

But if lack of compromise was a characteristic of the publishing house, it was a mark as well of their new author. On September 9, 1894, Crane responded to a suggestion that certain poems be omitted from the volume with a frosty refusal:

> In the first place I should absolutely refuse to have my poems printed without many of those which you just as absolutely mark "No." It seems to me that you cut all the ethical sense out of the book. All the anarchy, perhaps. It is the anarchy which I particularly insist upon. From the poems which you keep you could produce what might be termed a "nice little volume of verse by Stephen Crane," but for me there would be no satisfaction. The ones which refer to God, I believe you condemn altogether. I am obliged to have them in when my book is printed.[20]

Of course Crane was in a poorer position than Copeland & Day to be uncompromising: he was nearly unknown; they were established as leaders in their field. It is conceivable that Howells was asked to mediate the dispute, for the letter in which he predicted the demise of the prose-poem might be read as a gentle suggestion that Crane come to his senses. But it is not really necessary to posit any such intervention:

[19] Barry was at Harvard from 1884 to 1889; Copeland from 1887 to 1891. Elbert Hubbard briefly attended then too, and so did Herbert S. Stone and Hannibal Ingalls Kimball, founders of Stone & Kimball, who are supposed to have considered publishing *The Black Riders and Other Lines* and who did publish Crane later in *The Chap-Book*. See Sidney Kramer, *A History of Stone & Kimball and Herbert S. Stone & Co.* (Chicago, 1940), p. 21.

[20] September 9, 1894; in *Letters,* pp. 39–40.

although Crane could insist on having his own way, he was realist enough to know when he must submit.

Copeland & Day redefined their position in a note that has about it an air of finality; their strategy was to draw a firm line, suggest that Crane had the option of withdrawing his manuscript, and hold before him graphic evidence that the designing of the book would proceed only if he would submit at once:

Dear Sir:

We hope you will pardon this delay regarding your verses now with us, and beg to say that we will be glad to publish them if you will agree to omitting those beginning as follows.

1. A god it is said,
   Marked a sparrow's fall
2.[d] To the maiden
   The sea was a laughing meadow
3.[d] A god came to a man
   And spoke in this wise.
4.th There was a man with a tongue of wood.
5.th The traveller paused in kindness
6.th Should you stuff me with flowers
7.th One came from the skies.

Should you still object to omitting so many we will rest content to print all but the first three in the above list, though all of them appear to us as *far* better left unprinted.

We are sending by post a couple of drawings either of which might please you to be used by way of fronticepiece for the book; one would be something illustrative, while the other would be symbolic in a wide sense.

As to a title for the book, the one you suggest is acceptable if nothing better occurs to you. The omission of titles for separate poems is an idea we most heartily agree with.

We are also sending a blank form to receive your signature should you decide to entrust the book to our hands: a duplicate will be sent to you upon the return of this copy.

Kindly let us hear from you at as early a date as possible.[21]

[21] October 19, 1894; from the original in the Alderman Library, University of Virginia. Not in *Letters*.

Crane's reply was a curt note of capitulation enclosing a copy of the title poem—"Black riders came from the sea" (*1*)—and recording his latest change of address.[22] His book appeared without the seven poems proscribed by Copeland & Day. Three of those seven are now unknown, but four survive. Crane included "To the maiden the sea was blue meadow" (*78*) and "There was a man with tongue of wood" (*91*) in *War Is Kind,* the collection of his poems which was published four years later; Cora Crane attempted to print an edition of Stephen's poems that would have contained "One came from the skies" (*119*) and "A god came to a man and said to him thus" (*120*), but failed. They were first printed in 1957, inaccurately.[23]

Crane's complaint that his publishers wished to "cut all the ethical sense out of the book" is supported by the omissions. Although the title *The Black Riders and Other Lines* suggests that the volume is little more than a miscellany on the order of the later *War Is Kind,* it is actually a coherent whole. Crane apparently had anticipated his comment to John Northern Hilliard in a letter to *Leslie's Weekly:* "My aim was to comprehend in it the thoughts I have had about life in general." [24] The first and last poems form an envelope around these thoughts about life in general. "Black riders

[22] October 30, 1894; in *Letters,* p. 40. See also two letters not in *Letters:* Dean H. Keller, "Stephen Crane to Copeland & Day: A New Letter," and Joseph Katz, "Copeland & Day to Stephen Crane: A New Letter," *Stephen Crane Newsletter,* II (Fall 1967), 7–8. Crane changed his address frequently during this period. In April and May, for example, his letters bore a return address that varied from 111 West Thirty-third Street, to Camp Interlaken, Pennsylvania, to his brother's house at Hartwood, New York, and back to 143 East Twenty-third Street. He was poor, and roomed wherever he could.

[23] I identified Cora's edition in "Cora Crane and the Poetry of Stephen Crane," *Papers of the Bibliographical Society of America,* LVIII (Fourth Quarter 1964), 469–76. Poems *119* and *120* appeared first in Hoffman, *The Poetry of Stephen Crane.*

[24] See note 1, above. Yoshie Itabashi, "The Modern Pilgrimage of *The Black Riders:* An Interpretation," *Tsuda Review,* No. 12 (November 1967), pp. 1–41, carried the ideas which follow into an interpretation of the book as an expression of Darwinian thought.

came from the sea" (*1*), a suggestion of the Apocalypse and of the rider carrying the balances, serves as invocation to a muse of truth; and "A spirit sped through spaces of night" (*68*) ironically exposes God's trick on the soothsayer. In the center of that frame there is a coherent persona. In the parable-like poems, life is seen to be absurd; in the lyrics, it is implied that for life to be worthwhile despite its absurdities, it must revolve around human love. That the absurdity of life will make love always imperfect does not, in the world of *The Black Riders,* reduce the individual significance of either. These themes are central to Crane's poetry and form the basis of his esthetic.

The surviving four omitted poems indicate the path taken by "the ride of Sin." "A god came to a man" is a version of the temptation of Adam in which the deity confronts man directly. Here, man responds with the standard refutation of the doctrine of predestination: God has created man with his appetites and his weaknesses; if man could surmount these limitations, he would become greater than God. Actually, as the tone of "Adam's" response suggests, the power to construct such an argument places man above God. In "One came from the skies," Christ's divinity is slighted by the addition of "—They said—" (the lining is significant here as in all the poems), and the sacrament of marriage is repudiated.

In the context of *The Black Riders,* the remaining two omitted poems also would have taken on connotations of blasphemy.

"To the Maiden," in addition to being a "point of view" poem of the kind for which Thomas Wentworth Higginson praised Crane,[25] opposes the maiden's shallow romanticism with a view of Nature's capricious malignancy. It anticipated

[25] "Recent Poetry," *The Nation,* LXI (October 24, 1896), 296. For a discussion of Higginson on Crane, see my "The 'Preceptor' and Another Poet: Thomas Wentworth Higginson and Stephen Crane," *Serif,* V (March 1968), 17–21.

Crane's later stress on the utter indifference of the universe to the fate of the individual. "There was a man with tongue of wood" is less obviously recognized as destroying the notion of a guided universe. On the one hand this is the kind of self-reflexive irony of which Crane was fond, and the excessive "clip-clopping" of the version read by Copeland & Day might have offended their ears. But on the other hand, the poem can be read as the defiant dedication of an iconoclastic book to the Ikon, which might have offended them more.

Despite the omissions, the contract was signed and the details of publication were arranged quickly. Crane had already decided on the title of the book and on the publication of the poems without individual titles (a practice he affirmed in the periodical publications of his poems); he rejected Copeland & Day's suggestion that they use black-letter type, and settled with them on simple, Roman capitals, the poems all to begin on new pages, and to be identified by Roman numerals.[26] It was a peculiar presentation, one that quickly became Crane's poetic trademark, the most obvious trait to critics and reviewers who were either unable or unwilling to proceed further in their analyses. In a last-minute flurry, Crane arranged for Frederic C. Gordon to submit an orchid motif for the binding, and for the book to be dedicated to Hamlin Garland. On May 11, 1895, about seven months after the contract for it was signed, *The Black Riders and Other Lines* appeared. Stephen Crane had at last published a book. He was a poet, and he awaited word of his reception.

[26] Crane to Copeland & Day, December 10, 1894; in *Letters*, p. 42: "I have grown somewhat frightened at the idea of old English type since some of my recent encounters with it have made me think I was working out a puzzle." But in another letter to the publishers (December 16, 1894; in *Letters*, p. 42) he obviously is approving the format that finally was used: "The type, the page, the classic form of the sample suits me. It is however paragraphed wrong. There should be none."

The publication date of *The Black Riders and Other Lines* was no red letter day; it made little difference to anyone but Crane and his supporters. If it is a distortion to say with Thomas Beer that "the reading nation was told at once that Stephen Crane was mad," it would be almost equally wrong to agree with Thomas F. O'Donnell's suggestion that the book's reception was enthusiastic.[27] As one might expect of a first book of poems by an unknown, the reading nation was told very little at once. First comments came from those in the Howells-Garland-Barry camp, and subsequent remarks were made by their opponents. *The Black Riders* attracted notice initially for its associations and later for its achievements. When the phenomenal sales of *The Red Badge of Courage* brought Crane forth as the center of two public controversies, the poetry became of wider interest and was frequently reviewed in the context of the popularity of the novel.[28] But if the early comments are only minimally significant as an index of the book's popularity, they are of major importance because of their influence on the ways in which it was discussed.

For example, the strange format combined with the anti-traditional style and statement of the poems to suggest that *The Black Riders* resulted from an intentionally eccentric posture of the poet. Harvey Wickham called it "something

[27] Beer, *Stephen Crane,* p. 120; O'Donnell, "A Note on the Reception of Crane's *The Black Riders,*" *American Literature,* XXIV (May 1952), 233–35.

[28] The first is directly related to the novel. Some readers claimed that only a Civil War veteran could have written it. Among them were those who said that, therefore, its view of courage was a libel and a betrayal of them by one of their own, linking this through some strange logic to the English claim that Americans read the book only after the old country praised it. The second controversy was personal, of public interest only because the novel was in the news. Crane's bohemianism came to be noticed, leading to a suspicion of his morals that would be the background to charges of sexual misbehavior, narcotics addiction, and alcoholism later on, during his bungles in the Dora Clark affair. See Olov W. Fryckstedt, "Stephen Crane in the Tenderloin," *Studia Neophilologica,* XXXIV (1962), 135–63.

odd to attract attention." What was actually the mordant expression of Crane's dissatisfaction with the religious traditions of his family and his culture appeared to many to be well within the stream of Wilde, Beardsley, and the decadents. Thus, even though the influential *Bookman* threw its weight on Crane's side, it began the review by calling him "the Aubrey Beardsley of poetry":

When one first takes up his little book of verse and notes the quite too Beardsleyesque splash of black upon its staring white boards, and then on opening it discovers that the "lines" are printed wholly in capitals, and that they are unrhymed and destitute of what most poets regard as rhythm, the general impression is of a writer who is bidding for renown wholly on the basis of his eccentricity. But just as Mr. Beardsley with all his absurdities is none the less a master of black and white, so Mr. Crane is a true poet whose verse, long after the eccentricity of its form has worn off, fascinates us and forbids us to lay the volume down until the last line has been read.[29]

Although Professor Peck concluded that Crane was not a decadent but a "bold—sometimes too bold—original, and powerful writer of eccentric verse, skeptical, pessimistic, often cynical," the tactic provided a tag for contemporary reviewers and a vision for some later critics.[30]

A comparison between Crane and Walt Whitman was as immediate and certainly as inevitable as that with the decadents. "In fact," said the *Bookman,* "if Walt Whitman had been caught young and subjected to aesthetic influences, it is likely that he would have mellowed his barbaric yawp to some such note as that which sounds in the poems before us." [31] Despite the direct protest of Horace Traubel's *Con-*

[29] Harry Thurston Peck, "Some Recent Volumes of Verse," *Bookman,* I (May 1895), 254.

[30] The label of decadence still clings, although it has been modified into a loose, almost meaningless, tag in such a comment as "there are *decadent* qualities in Stephen Crane"—W. F. Thrall, Addison Hibbard, and C. H. Holman, *A Handbook to Literature* (New York, 1960), p. 131.

[31] Peck, "Some Recent Volumes of Verse," p. 254.

servator, an organ devoted to the outpourings of the Whitman apostles at the time, contemporary reviewers considered this comparison valid and useful.[32] Usually, however, Crane suffered in the measure. Jeanette L. Gilder, for example, sternly said, "We may have pardoned Walt Whitman's shortcoming in this direction for the sake of his poetic thoughts, but we cannot go on forgiving these eccentricities of genius forever." [33]

But not all comments on *The Black Riders* were serious attempts at definition or criticism. The nineties were gay in many ways, perhaps gayest in embracing parody and satire of the kind which now seems sophomoric, and Crane's book was the target of fun both friendly and vicious. Its format was extravagant, its style and images equally so; *The Black Riders* must have seemed to the humorists and would-be humorists an heaven-sent gift for their wit. Even the enthusiastic *Bookman* followed extravagant praise with a parody beginning "I explain the crooked track of a coon at night"; little wonder then that Crane jokes abounded, caricatures of Crane riding strange beasts flourished, and Elbert Hubbard —soon to feast Crane—might even have been trying to puff the book in his own way: [34]

Messrs. Copeland & Day of Boston recently published for Mr. Stephen Crane a book which he called "The Black Riders." I don't know why; the riders might have as easily been green or yellow or baby-blue for all the book tells about them, and I think the title "The Pink Roosters" would have been better, but

[32] Isaac Hull Plat, "The Black Riders," *Conservator,* VI (July 1895), 78; reprinted in my "Whitman, Crane, and the Odious Comparison," *Notes and Queries,* n.s. XIV (February 1967), 66–67.

[33] Gilder, "Stephen Crane's Study of War," New York *World,* February 23, 1896, p. 18, considers Crane's poetry in the course of reviewing *The Red Badge of Courage.* Notably different, however, is the position of the reviewer for the London *Times,* February 4, 1897, p. 7.

[34] W. S. Bean, "Lines after Stephen Crane," *Bookman,* IV (December 1896), 332; Hubbard, *Philistine,* I (June 1895), 27.

it doesn't matter. My friend, The Onlooker, of *Town Topics,* quotes one of the verses and says this, which I heartily endorse:

> I saw a man pursuing the horizon;
> Round and round they sped.
> I was disturbed at this;
> I accosted the man.
> "It is futile," I said,
> "You can never"—
> "You lie," he cried,
> And ran on.

This was Mr. Howells proving that Ibsen is valuable and interesting. It is to be hoped that Mr. Crane will write another poem about him after his legs have been worn off.

Strange to say, six months later Hubbard invited Crane to accept a dinner in his honor, and six months after that he inaugurated a new periodical with a commemoration of that dinner—and the first poem in that issue was the very one he had ridiculed in his review. Perhaps stranger still, even while Crane was regularly contributing to the *Philistine,* Hubbard was ready to devote a page to Crane's verse, to puffing it, or to parodying it.

Despite the sparse mixture of reviews that greeted *The Black Riders and Other Lines,* Crane soon earned the reputation of being "a wonderful boy." While he had been negotiating for the book of poetry, *The Red Badge of Courage* had been syndicated in the newspapers (in much abbreviated form), and the immediate attention gained earned it a contract with D. Appleton and Company.[35] Reviewers frequently looked back on the poems with disdain, but they did look back. And as sales of *The Red Badge of Courage* soared, Crane's name became marketable.

[35] See Joseph Katz, "*The Red Badge of Courage*" (Gainesville, Florida, 1967), for a study of the version of the novel distributed by the Bacheller and Johnson Syndicate in December 1894.

So perhaps it is not surprising that Elbert Hubbard, the man who has been called "the founder of modern American advertising," was one of the first to jump on the Crane bandwagon and offer him a steady outlet for his poems.[36] Though the *Philistine* of July 1895 had printed a parody of his poetic technique, the August and September issues carried two poems (*94* and *101*) that Copeland & Day apparently had not seen. This might seem a break between Crane and the *avant garde* Hubbard opposed (and with which Crane had been identified). Amy Lowell, for example, recoiled at the association with Fra Elbertus: "It was difficult for the world to believe that a man championed by the arch-poser, Elbert Hubbard, could have merit." [37] But the road to success makes for strange companions, and Hubbard did share a common inspiration with Copeland & Day, Stone & Kimball, the early *Bookman* people, and the other Crane enthusiasts.

Early in the last decade of the nineteenth century, Hubbard had visited William Morris and England. In the words of Felix Shay, Hubbard's employee and biographer,

> When Hubbard came a-visiting, Morris was getting on toward sixty, while Hubbard was still in his middle thirties. The difference in ages made it easy for one to give and the other to take; one, in a sense, became the apostle of the other. Morris tossed the torch to the hand that was ready to grasp it, and Hubbard said he "caught it!" [38]

If his grasp was faulty, there was still something of the theories and ideals of Morris surrounding Hubbard's early

[36] For discussions of Hubbard's publication of Crane, see David H. Dickason, "Stephen Crane and the *Philistine*," *American Literature*, XV (November 1943), 279–87; and Simeon Braunstein, "A Checklist of Writings by and about Stephen Crane in *The Fra*," *Stephen Crane Newsletter*, III (Winter 1968), 8. Their relationship is tracked through their correspondence, most of it first published, in my "How Elbert Hubbard Met Stephen Crane," *Stephen Crane Newsletter*, II (Spring 1968), 8–12. And Hubbard's private opinion of Crane's poetry is in my "Elbert Hubbard to Lyman Chandler: A Note on Crane's Poetic," *Stephen Crane Newsletter*, III (Fall 1968), 8–9.

[37] *The Work of Stephen Crane*, Wilson Follett, ed. (New York, 1926), VI, xxiii.

[38] Shay, *Elbert Hubbard of East Aurora* (New York, 1926), p. 31.

operations. Despite his failure to "grasp the fundamentals of this thought," [39] he did have an influence on the *kultur* of his day, and an influence as well on Crane's career.

" 'East Aurora,' said Hubbard, 'is not a place; it's a state of mind.' " [40] That state of mind transformed a small, upper New York state village into the Roycroft community, a group of moderately skillful artificers who produced mission style furniture, and who designed, printed, occasionally illuminated, and bound books that aped the Kelmscott Press works.[41] A survey of the Roycroft Press output easily determines the center of the East Aurora world: a few titles were first printings of authors discovered by Hubbard, many were reprintings of the classics and near-classics, but most were publications of the writings of Elbert Hubbard. These last maintained just the right posture of staid and limited bohemianism that would pique the interest of the slightly daring businessman.

And these characteristics of the Hubbard touch are apparent in the most successful of the Roycroft ventures, the *Philistine*. Purporting to be the organ of a Society of the Philistines, the periodical was begun in June 1895, evidently in response to the newly-begun San Francisco *Lark*. The majority of its contents were monthly comments on life and the arts in a tone of which the review of *The Black Riders* is representative. But Hubbard quickly saw in Crane a cause and a good thing, and he invited him to be guest of honor at a hastily formed first annual dinner of the Society of the Philistines.

"Recognizing in yourself and in your genius as a poet, a man who we would like to know better," the invitation

[39] James D. Hart, *The Oxford Companion to American Literature,* Third Edition (New York, 1966), p. 342.

[40] Shay, *Elbert Hubbard of East Aurora,* p. 53.

[41] Theodore Dreiser recorded his disgust with Hubbard in *A Hoosier Holiday* (New York, 1916), pp. 141–44, 163–68. After a few hours in East Aurora, Dreiser fled. But I am no longer sure that I have been fair to Hubbard's place in American culture in what I have said about him here.

began, "The Society of the Philistines desires to give a dinner in your honor early in the future." "I was very properly enraged at the word 'poet' which continually reminds me of long-hair and seems to be to be a most detestable form of insult but nevertheless I replied," Crane recalled.[42] Naïvely, he wondered if the honor came because he had written "for their magazine" and was overwhelmed by feelings of "pride and arrogance to think that I have such friends." [43] But December 19, 1895, greeted him with something that was not quite a fête. Although Hubbard had declared Crane a "cause" and stated that the Philistines wished "in a dignified, public (and at the same time) elegant manner to recognize that cause," Crane stood in borrowed clothing to be roasted by a gathering of what one guest described as "freaks or near-freaks." [44]

Shocked, a guest stood up to leave, but he was stopped by Crane and Willis Brooks Hawkins, a friend and benefactor. This submersion of dignity was undoubtedly wise: Hubbard continued to provide a steady outlet for Crane's work. For the dinner, for example, he issued elaborate souvenir menus —*"The Time Has Come," The Walrus Said, "To Talk of Many Things"*—first publishing "I have heard the sunset song of the birches" (*82*), and several months later began *The Roycroft Quarterly* with a souvenir of the occasion, *A Souvenir and a Medley*. The latter publication allowed

[42] The invitation and Crane's summary of the event are in Edwin H. Cady and Lester G. Wells, eds., *Stephen Crane's Love Letters to Nellie Crouse* (Syracuse, 1954), pp. 25–27.

[43] Crane to Willis Brooks Hawkins, [November 15, 1895], [November 12, 1895]; in *Letters,* pp. 74, 73.

[44] Hubbard to Crane, November 16, 1895; in *Letters,* p. 76. Frank Noxon's report of "freaks and near-freaks" is in Cady and Wells, *Love Letters to Nellie Crouse,* pp. 63–69. Claude F. Bragdon's "The Purple Cow Period," *Bookman,* LXIX (July 1928), 478, supports his view. Willis Brooks Hawkins, however, took another one; it is in my " 'Stephen Crane Flinches'," *Stephen Crane Newsletter,* III (Fall 1968), 6–7. These men all were there. What probably happened was that Hubbard's dinner was in the nature of a Friar's Club roast, honoring the guest by treating him to good-natured fun of a rough kind.

Hubbard to get double mileage out of Crane's work: the six poems that had appeared in the *Philistine* to that time were reprinted, and the June *Philistine* printing of "Fast rode the knight" (*83*) was anticipated.

In all, Hubbard published twenty-one of Crane's poems (many more than once) and was Crane's major periodical outlet for them. The bulk of publication took place in the period August 1895–June 1896; there was a lapse between July 1896 and January 1898; and further poems appeared between February 1898 and October 1898, with reprintings through 1899. The lapse may be explained in part by Crane's travels, in part by the development of other, more congenial outlets (the *Bookman* and Stone & Kimball's *Chap-Book*) for his poems, in part by Hubbard's "democratic prejudice against royalties," [45] and in part by Hubbard's lack of taste, his deficient understanding of the nature of literary art, his "editing" Crane's work to suit himself, and his grotesque use of a famous near-tragedy as an occasion for advertisement. On January 1, 1897, Crane was on the *Commodore* when it mysteriously sank while carrying arms and ammunition to Cuban rebels. He was missing until January 3, and was thought dead. The proximity to death scarred him, and he attempted to write his experience out in "Stephen Crane's Own Story," "The Open Boat," and "Flanagan and His Short Filibustering Adventure." These scars show even more lividly in his use of the sea in his poems, especially in "A Man Adrift on a Slim Spar" (*113*). At best, Hubbard was insensitive to how a brush with death might have affected Crane. In the *Philistine* of February 1897 he printed a lachrymose obituary on Crane's drowning, following it a few pages after by "LATER: Thanks to Providence and a hen-

[45] Frank Noxon (in Cady and Wells, *Love Letters to Nellie Crouse,* p. 69) characterized Hubbard's attitude to payment for contributions. Hubbard's letters to Crane in "How Elbert Hubbard Met Stephen Crane" (see note 36, above) clearly say that the poems would have to be donated in return for publicity. And Crane evidently agreed to the game.

coop, Steve Crane was not drowned after all—he swam ashore."

Although neither the *Chap-Book,* with its one Crane poem, nor the *Bookman,* with its twelve (two reprinted from *The Black Riders,* and three first printed posthumously), approach the bulk published by Hubbard, they are significant indications of the appeal of Crane's work. During the editorship of Harry Thurston Peck, then a professor of Latin at Columbia University, the *Bookman* was an artistically advanced, if politically conservative, literary journal. Nevertheless, and no doubt under Peck's direction, the periodical boosted Crane shamelessly. In addition to avowed, and usually favorable, reviews "Chronicle and Comment" occasionally dropped Crane's name before its readers. On the first page of the March 1896 number, for example, *Bookman* slammed *Jude the Obscure* by suggesting "In the Desert" (*3*) as its epigraph. But the chief value of the *Bookman* and the *Chap-Book* to Crane was probably their assurance that discriminating journals found his poems acceptable. And this assurance could only have been strengthened by an occasional reprinting in the New York *Times,* in the numerous literary digests, and in such a mass-circulation anthology as Sidney A. Witherbee's *Spanish-American War Songs.*

If one adds this substantial periodical success to Crane's "Personally, I like my little book of poems, 'The Black Riders,' better than I do 'The Red Badge of Courage'," one must conclude that he was a committed poet forging his way. So some bewilderment is natural when one realizes that only a very small body of verse survives. To a degree the slimness of the canon can be explained by Crane's carelessness. After Crane's death, Cora Crane received "All-Feeling God, Hear in the War-Night" (*129*) with a note from Charles Michelson explaining that he found it in Crane's discarded Spanish-American War saddle-bags.[46] But there are other, more important reasons for a small poetic output.

[46] Lillian Gilkes, *Cora Crane* (Bloomington, Indiana, 1960), p. 288n.

When William Dean Howells attempted to dissuade Crane from writing the "prose poem," when he remarked on the "simple, but always most graphic" terms in which *Maggie* was expressed, and when he made a point by printing one of the poems in *The Black Riders* as prose, he was gesturing toward Crane's exceptional ability to bring the rhythms of prose and poetry close.[47] For if Crane was not entirely satisfied to "quench the old rage and satisfy the old commitment in stories," [48] he was able to integrate into his fiction the esthetic, themes, and rhythms on which his poetry depends. The parallel suggested by Howells was extended more significantly by Melvin Schoberlin's printing of excerpts from the early prose as poetry.[49] But even though Crane could draw the rhythmic modes together, and could use themes and episodes as well and better in his fiction as in the poems, it was the burning need of money rather than the quenching of artistic rage that assured a small poetic output.[50]

[47] *Letters,* p. 40; "New York Low Life in Fiction," New York *World,* July 26, 1896, p. 18, and "An Appreciation" in *Maggie: A Child of the Streets* (London, 1896); "Life and Letters," *Harper's Weekly,* XL (January 25, 1896), 79.

[48] Morgan Blum, "Berryman as Biographer, Stephen Crane as Poet," *Poetry,* LXXVIII (August 1951), 307.

[49] *The Sullivan County Sketches of Stephen Crane* (Syracuse, 1949), p. 13.

[50] The duplication of incident in the poetry and prose has not yet been sufficiently explored. Perhaps the most striking of these twins is a vignette in *Maggie* and in "With Eye and With Gesture" (*57*). In the novelette, Pete brushes away Maggie's "But where kin I go?" with "Oh, go teh hell!" The girl walks the streets, distraught:

> Suddenly she came upon a stout gentleman in a silk hat and a chaste black coat, whose decorous row of buttons reached from his chin to his knees. The girl had heard of the Grace of God and she decided to approach this man.
>
> His beaming, chubby face was a picture of benevolence and kind-heartedness. His eyes shone good-will.
>
> But as the girl timidly accosted him, he gave a convulsive movement and saved his respectability by a vigorous side-step. He did not risk it to save a soul. For how was he to know that there was a soul before him that needed saving? (1893, pp. 141–42.)

H. G. Wells's horror at "a medley of disproportionate expenditure" displayed by the Cranes at a Brede Place Christmas party is indicative of the shameful waste of time, energy, and money in which Cora and Stephen indulged.[51] In an attempt to keep but slightly behind his debts, Crane ground out short stories at a phenomenal rate, forcing his English agent to plead for a diminishment of the pressure to sell, sell, sell: "There is a risk of spoiling the market if we have to dump too many short stories on it at once," the man protested.[52] But Crane stepped up the pressure, and Pinker's prediction came true: as Crane flooded the market with his work, his rate of pay dwindled.[53] And still the mill ground faster and worse.

The sheer bulk of the short fiction eventually looked to overwhelm the gradually fewer pieces of quality, and did of course overwhelm the poetry. Poetry did not bring in money. Ironically, the dwindling number of poems allows the direction of Crane's later poetry to come into clearer focus. It had always been dramatic in conception. The journey motif of *The Black Riders* is essentially a dramatic concept, and the poems for which that motif provides continuity are dramatic in structure. Crane made frequent gestures to-

The incident is compressed and the judgment explicit in the poem:

> With eye and with gesture
> You say you are holy.
> I say you lie;
> For I did see you
> Draw away your coats
> From the sin upon the hands
> Of a little child.
> Liar!

[51] *Experiment in Autobiography* (New York, 1934), p. 524.

[52] James B. Pinker to Crane, October 24, 1899; in *Letters*, p. 236.

[53] James B. Stronks has discussed Crane as an earner in "Stephen Crane's English Years: The Legend Corrected," *Papers of the Bibliographical Society of America*, LVII (Third Quarter 1963), 340–49. See also Matthew J. Bruccoli and Joseph Katz, "Scholarship and Mere Artifacts: The British and Empire Publications of Stephen Crane," *Studies in Bibliography*, XXII (1969), 277–87.

ward writing for the stage; although they culminated disappointingly in *The Ghost,* they produced pieces as interesting as "A Prologue" and are relevant to a discussion of his esthetic.[54]

As in his plays, his sketches, and his scenes, many of the poems Crane wrote for *The Black Riders* depend on a clash of voices. Thomas Wentworth Higginson had praised the book for offering "points-of-view" of a situation, and in saying this he was pointing at a technique of dramatic interplay. Frequently there is a major voice, usually that of the

[54] In September, 1895, Crane thought he would be doing drama criticism for the Philadelphia *Press,* but the job offer was withdrawn (see *Letters,* p. 63). There is, nevertheless, a body of criticism of the stage and its environment: "Some Hints for Play Makers," "Miss Louise Gerard—Soprano," "Grand Opera in New Orleans," "Mardi Gras Festival," and "At the Pit Door." These were all published in Crane's lifetime and are reprinted in Olov W. Fryckstedt, ed., *Stephen Crane: Uncollected Writings* (Uppsala, 1963).

There was a playwriting career as well. In 1896, according to Thomas Beer, *Stephen Crane,* p. 13, Crane planned to collaborate on a play with Clyde Fitch. At about the same time, Crane wrote Nellie Crouse (see Cady and Wells, *Love Letters to Nellie Crouse,* pp. 97–98) that a Boston theater owner had asked him to write a play for him. Joseph Conrad recalled (Beer, pp. 29–30) Crane's eagerness for a collaboration on a play to be called *The Predecessor:*

> The general subject consisted in a man personating his "predecessor" (who had died) in the hope of winning a girl's heart. The scenes were to include a ranch at the foot of the Rocky Mountains, I remember, and the action I fear would have been frankly melodramatic. Crane insisted that one of the situations should present the man and the girl on a boundless plain standing by their dead ponies after a furious ride (a truly Crane touch). I made some objections. A boundless plain in the light of a sunset could be got into a back-cloth, I admitted; but I doubted whether we could induce the management of any London theatre to deposit two stuffed horses on its stage.

But Crane did not shrug off the dramatic urge.

In addition to the ironic "The Blood of the Martyr" (Frychkstedt, *Uncollected Writings,* pp. 309–14), there is the unpublished "The Ghost," an entertainment performed at Brede Place for Christmas, 1899, the unpublished first act of a play set in a French tavern, and a play posthumously published in R. W. Stallman and E. R. Hagemann, eds., *The War Dispatches of Stephen Crane* (New York, 1964), pp. 318–34, as "Drama in Cuba."

persona, reporting an incident seen ("In the desert | I saw a creature, naked, bestial" *3*), retailed ("Once there came a man | Who said: | 'Range me all men of the world in rows' " *5*), or experienced ("A learned man came to me once" *20*). The second voice and occasionally the other voices represent a point of view which is revealed as inferior. In this clash, a dominant attitude emerges. "Preaching is fatal to art in literature," Crane had said self-consciously to John Northern Hilliard. "I try to give readers a slice out of life; and if there is any moral or lesson in it, I do not try to point it out. I let the reader find it for himself. The result is more satisfactory to both the reader and myself." [55] The failures in *The Black Riders* might well be attributed to the occasional harshness with which the dominant attitude is developed.

While Crane retained the dramatic device in many of the later poems, he gained a sufficiently tight control of the technique to subdue the "preachiness." The epigrammatic "A man said to the universe" (*96*) echoes effectively not because the poem is simple, but because the dramatic interplay is precise and economical. This sophistication—sophistication in the best sense—was extended in Crane's experimentation with a functionally dramatic refrain and with the dramatic opposition of stanzas. On the surface this might appear to be but a movement from a parable tradition into the highly formal structures characteristic of the contemporary mainstream; in actuality it was an extension of Crane's experiments in integrating dramatic devices with poetry. As in "Do not weep, maiden, for war is kind" (*76*) and "All-feeling God, hear in the war-night" (*129*), the opposition of stanzas and the use of the refrain serve as a kind of choric undercutting of what is apparently the major statement. In these poems, the choric voice is consistent and the agonic voice diffuse; the result in the successful poems is a subtle irony that distinguishes *War Is Kind* from the early volume.

[55] Crane to Hilliard; quoted in "Stephen Crane" (see note 1, above).

But if Crane was at times able to submerge himself in his poetry in an attempt to retain the artistic satisfaction that he was frequently forced to relinquish in the prose, he was finally pushed to transmute the verse into money. This is the key to an otherwise puzzling volume. *The Black Riders* is distinguished by its coherence derived from an intensity of composition, and by the violently protective urge evident in the correspondence between Crane and Copeland & Day. In contrast, the aura surrounding *War Is Kind* partakes rather of gleaning than of sowing, and it is dominated by the careless off-handedness that Crane assumed in closing an affair of purely business interest. Frederick A. Stokes Company, through its London representative, had advanced Crane money, had made him outright loans, and had guaranteed several of his debts.[56] In what was obviously an attempt to repay this obligation, or at least to stave it off, he collected many of the poems that had appeared in the periodicals since the publication of *The Black Riders,* added a few he had on hand, padded with one that had been printed in the first book, and surrendered the agglomeration to Stokes as *War Is Kind.*

These commercial qualities are apparent in the contents of this second volume of Crane's poetry. Only the embarrassingly tedious "Intrigue" cycle and twelve of the poems in the major section of the book are first printings. Of the twelve, no more than nine could possibly have been written for *War Is Kind:* two (*78* and *91*) were among those rejected earlier by Copeland & Day, and a fragment of one (*79*) had been sent to Elbert Hubbard for the Philistine. The occasionally Whitmanesque "Intrigue" had been written while Crane was in Cuba in 1898, and had been offered to William Heinemann (Crane's English publisher) for separate publication.[57] But although Heinemann had published *The Black Riders*

[56] For example, Stokes had agreed to stand surety on a two-year-old debt. See Crane to Pinker, February 4, 1899; in *Letters,* pp. 207–208.

[57] Crane to Paul Revere Reynolds, October 20, 1898; in *Letters,* p. 189.

in a format that suggests respect for Crane's poetry, they declined "Intrigue." Crane reinforced the commercial air of the book by noting in his typescript the original appearance of each of the reprintings and, moreover—without noting that it had appeared in *The Black Riders*—used as a filler "There was one I met upon the road" (*33, 99*).

War Is Kind was copyrighted in April 1899 and announced for sale in May.[58] The tall, grey-paper volume shouted "decadence" at its audience, and reinforced the tag that had been applied to Crane four years earlier. Yet he almost certainly had no voice in selecting the format, no decision in the choice of Will Bradley, the illustrator whose Beardsleyesque black-and-whites guaranteed the *fin de siècle* atmosphere, and evidently no hand in correcting the proof of the book.

But Crane's life was dribbling away. When Edmund Clarence Stedman asked for some poems for inclusion in his important *American Anthology,* he had feebly responded to the honor with the incorrect statement that every poem he had ever written would be found in his two published volumes. In his concern with debt, the loss of satisfaction with the relation of his life and art, and his physical weakness, the young man who once had jibed at his wooden tongue was shattered into the parodist of Longfellow:

> Tell me not in joyous numbers
> We can make our lives sublime
> By—well, at least, not by
> Dabbling much in rhyme.

[58] Although Sidney Pawling of Heinemann had a script of *War Is Kind* under consideration as late as February 1899, the book was never published in England. Heinemann did use copies of the Stokes edition for English copyright deposit, however, in an arrangement that was common between cooperative transatlantic publishers. See Matthew J. Bruccoli and Joseph Katz, "The Heinemann *War Is Kind,*" *Stephen Crane Newsletter,* I (Spring 1967), 6.

The Black Riders
and Other Lines

1

Black riders came from the sea.
There was clang and clang of spear and shield,
And clash and clash of hoof and heel,
Wild shouts and the wave of hair
In the rush upon the wind:
Thus the ride of Sin.

2

Three little birds in a row
Sat musing.
A man passed near that place.
Then did the little birds nudge each other.

They said: "He thinks he can sing."
They threw back their heads to laugh.
With quaint countenances
They regarded him.
They were very curious,
Those three little birds in a row.

3

In the desert
I saw a creature, naked, bestial,
Who, squatting upon the ground,
Held his heart in his hands,
And ate of it.
I said: "Is it good, friend?"
"It is bitter—bitter," he answered;
"But I like it
Because it is bitter,
And because it is my heart."

4

Yes, I have a thousand tongues,
And nine and ninety-nine lie.
Though I strive to use the one,
It will make no melody at my will,
But is dead in my mouth.

5

Once there came a man
Who said:
"Range me all men of the world in rows."
And instantly
There was terrific clamor among the people
Against being ranged in rows.
There was a loud quarrel, world-wide.
It endured for ages;
And blood was shed
By those who would not stand in rows,
And by those who pined to stand in rows.
Eventually, the man went to death, weeping.
And those who stayed in bloody scuffle
Knew not the great simplicity.

6

God fashioned the ship of the world carefully.
With the infinite skill of an all-master
Made He the hull and the sails,
Held He the rudder
Ready for adjustment.
Erect stood He, scanning His work proudly.
Then—at fateful time—a wrong called,
And God turned, heeding.
Lo, the ship, at this opportunity, slipped slyly,
Making cunning noiseless travel down the ways.
So that, forever rudderless, it went upon the seas
Going ridiculous voyages,
Making quaint progress,
Turning as with serious purpose
Before stupid winds.
And there were many in the sky
Who laughed at this thing.

7

Mystic shadow, bending near me,
Who art thou?
Whence come ye?
And–tell me–is it fair
Or is the truth bitter as eaten fire?
Tell me!
Fear not that I should quaver,
For I dare–I dare.
Then, tell me!

8

I looked here;
I looked there;
Nowhere could I see my love.
And—this time—
She was in my heart.
Truly, then, I have no complaint,
For though she be fair and fairer,
She is none so fair as she
In my heart.

9

I stood upon a high place,
And saw, below, many devils
Running, leaping,
And carousing in sin.
One looked up, grinning,
And said: "Comrade! Brother!"

10

Should the wide world roll away,
Leaving black terror,
Limitless night,
Nor God, nor man, nor place to stand
Would be to me essential,
If thou and thy white arms were there,
And the fall to doom a long way.

11

In a lonely place,
I encountered a sage
Who sat, all still,
Regarding a newspaper.
He accosted me:
"Sir, what is this?"
Then I saw that I was greater,
Aye, greater than this sage.
I answered him at once:
"Old, old man, it is the wisdom of the age."
The sage looked upon me with admiration.

12 “And the sins of the fathers shall be visited upon the heads of the children, even unto the third and fourth generation of them that hate me.”

Well, then, I hate Thee, unrighteous picture;
Wicked image, I hate Thee;
So, strike with Thy vengeance
The heads of those little men
Who come blindly.
It will be a brave thing.

13

If there is a witness to my little life,
To my tiny throes and struggles,
He sees a fool;
And it is not fine for gods to menace fools.

14

There was crimson clash of war.
Lands turned black and bare;
Women wept;
Babes ran, wondering.
There came one who understood not these things.
He said: "Why is this?"
Whereupon a million strove to answer him.
There was such intricate clamor of tongues,
That still the reason was not.

15 "Tell brave deeds of war."

Then they recounted tales:
"There were stern stands
And bitter runs for glory."

Ah, I think there were braver deeds.

16

Charity, thou art a lie,
A toy of women,
A pleasure of certain men.
In the presence of justice,
Lo, the walls of the temple
Are visible
Through thy form of sudden shadows.

17

There were many who went in huddled procession,
They knew not whither;
But, at any rate, success or calamity
Would attend all in equality.

There was one who sought a new road.
He went into direful thickets,
And ultimately he died thus, alone;
But they said he had courage.

18

In Heaven,
Some little blades of grass
Stood before God.
"What did you do?"
Then all save one of the little blades
Began eagerly to relate
The merits of their lives.
This one stayed a small way behind,
Ashamed.
Presently, God said:
"And what did you do?"
The little blade answered: "Oh, my Lord,
Memory is bitter to me,
For, if I did good deeds,
I know not of them."
Then God, in all His splendor,
Arose from His throne.
"Oh, best little blade of grass!" He said.

19

A god in wrath
Was beating a man;
He cuffed him loudly
With thunderous blows
That rang and rolled over the earth.
All people came running.
The man screamed and struggled,
And bit madly at the feet of the god.
The people cried:
"Ah, what a wicked man!"
And–
"Ah, what a redoubtable god!"

20

A learned man came to me once.
He said: "I know the way,—come."
And I was overjoyed at this.
Together we hastened.
Soon, too soon, were we
Where my eyes were useless,
And I knew not the ways of my feet.
I clung to the hand of my friend;
But at last he cried: "I am lost."

21

There was, before me,
Mile upon mile
Of snow, ice, burning sand.
And yet I could look beyond all this,
To a place of infinite beauty;
And I could see the loveliness of her
Who walked in the shade of the trees.
When I gazed,
All was lost
But this place of beauty and her.
When I gazed,
And in my gazing, desired,
Then came again
Mile upon mile,
Of snow, ice, burning sand.

22

Once I saw mountains angry,
And ranged in battle-front.
Against them stood a little man;
Aye, he was no bigger than my finger.
I laughed, and spoke to one near me:
"Will he prevail?"
"Surely," replied this other;
"His grandfathers beat them many times."
Then did I see much virtue in grandfathers,–
At least, for the little man
Who stood against the mountains.

23

Places among the stars,
Soft gardens near the sun,
Keep your distant beauty;
Shed no beams upon my weak heart.
Since she is here
In a place of blackness,
Not your golden days
Nor your silver nights
Can call me to you.
Since she is here
In a place of blackness,
Here I stay and wait.

24

I saw a man pursuing the horizon;
Round and round they sped.
I was disturbed at this;
I accosted the man.
"It is futile," I said,
"You can never—"

"You lie," he cried,
And ran on.

25

Behold, the grave of a wicked man,
And near it, a stern spirit.

There came a drooping maid with violets,
But the spirit grasped her arm.
"No flowers for him," he said.
The maid wept:
"Ah, I loved him."
But the spirit, grim and frowning:
"No flowers for him."

Now, this is it—
If the spirit was just,
Why did the maid weep?

26

There was set before me a mighty hill,
And long days I climbed
Through regions of snow.
When I had before me the summit-view,
It seemed that my labor
Had been to see gardens
Lying at impossible distances.

27

A youth in apparel that glittered
Went to walk in a grim forest.
There he met an assassin
Attired all in garb of old days;
He, scowling through the thickets,
And dagger poised quivering,
Rushed upon the youth.
"Sir," said this latter,
"I am enchanted, believe me,
To die, thus,
In this medieval fashion,
According to the best legends;
Ah, what joy!"
Then took he the wound, smiling,
And died, content.

28

"Truth," said a traveller,
"Is a rock, a mighty fortress;
Often have I been to it,
Even to its highest tower,
From whence the world looks black."

"Truth," said a traveller,
"Is a breath, a wind,
A shadow, a phantom;
Long have I pursued it,
But never have I touched
The hem of its garment."

And I believed the second traveller;
For truth was to me
A breath, a wind,
A shadow, a phantom,
And never had I touched
The hem of its garment.

29

Behold, from the land of the farther suns
I returned.
And I was in a reptile-swarming place,
Peopled, otherwise, with grimaces,
Shrouded above in black impenetrableness.
I shrank, loathing,
Sick with it.
And I said to him:
"What is this?"
He made answer slowly:
"Spirit, this is a world;
This was your home."

30

Supposing that I should have the courage
To let a red sword of virtue
Plunge into my heart,
Letting to the weeds of the ground
My sinful blood,
What can you offer me?
A gardened castle?
A flowery kingdom?

What? A hope?
Then hence with your red sword of virtue.

31

Many workmen
Built a huge ball of masonry
Upon a mountain-top.
Then they went to the valley below,
And turned to behold their work.
"It is grand," they said;
They loved the thing.

Of a sudden, it moved:
It came upon them swiftly;
It crushed them all to blood.
But some had opportunity to squeal.

32

Two or three angels
Came near to the earth.
They saw a fat church.
Little black streams of people
Came and went in continually.
And the angels were puzzled
To know why the people went thus,
And why they stayed so long within.

33

There was One I met upon the road
Who looked at me with kind eyes.
He said: "Show me of your wares."
And I did,
Holding forth one.
He said: "It is a sin."
Then I held forth another.
He said: "It is a sin."
Then I held forth another.
He said: "It is a sin."
And so to the end.
Always He said: "It is a sin."
At last, I cried out:
"But I have none other."
He looked at me
With kinder eyes.
"Poor soul," He said.

34

I stood upon a highway,
And, behold, there came
Many strange pedlers.
To me each one made gestures,
Holding forth little images, saying:
"This is my pattern of God.
Now this is the God I prefer."

But I said: "Hence!
Leave me with mine own,
And take you yours away;
I can't buy of your patterns of God,
The little gods you may rightly prefer."

35

A man saw a ball of gold in the sky;
He climbed for it,
And eventually he achieved it—
It was clay.

Now this is the strange part:
When the man went to the earth
And looked again,
Lo, there was the ball of gold.
Now this is the strange part:
It was a ball of gold.
Aye, by the heavens, it was a ball of gold.

36

I met a seer.
He held in his hands
The book of wisdom.
"Sir," I addressed him,
"Let me read."
"Child—" he began.
"Sir," I said,
"Think not that I am a child,
For already I know much
Of that which you hold.
Aye, much."

He smiled.
Then he opened the book
And held it before me.—
Strange that I should have grown so suddenly blind.

37 On the horizon the peaks assembled;
And as I looked,
The march of the mountains began.
As they marched, they sang:
"Aye! We come! We come!"

38 The ocean said to me once:
"Look!
Yonder on the shore
Is a woman, weeping.
I have watched her.
Go you and tell her this,—
Her lover I have laid
In cool green hall.
There is wealth of golden sand
And pillars, coral-red;
Two white fish stand guard at his bier.

"Tell her this
And more,—
That the king of the seas
Weeps too, old, helpless man.
The bustling fates
Heap his hands with corpses
Until he stands like a child
With surplus of toys."

39

The livid lightnings flashed in the clouds;
The leaden thunders crashed.
A worshipper raised his arm.
"Hearken! Hearken! The voice of God!"

"Not so," said a man.
"The voice of God whispers in the heart
So softly
That the soul pauses,
Making no noise,
And strives for these melodies,
Distant, sighing, like faintest breath,
And all the being is still to hear."

40 And you love me?

I love you.

You are, then, cold coward.

Aye; but, beloved,
When I strive to come to you,
Man's opinions, a thousand thickets,
My interwoven existence,
My life,
Caught in the stubble of the world
Like a tender veil,—
This stays me.
No strange move can I make
Without noise of tearing.
I dare not.

If love loves,
There is no world
Nor word.
All is lost
Save thought of love
And place to dream.
You love me?

I love you.

You are, then, cold coward.

Aye; but, beloved—

41

Love walked alone.
The rocks cut her tender feet,
And the brambles tore her fair limbs.
There came a companion to her,
But, alas, he was no help,
For his name was Heart's Pain.

42

I walked in a desert.
And I cried:
"Ah, God, take me from this place!"
A voice said: "It is no desert."
I cried: "Well, but—
The sand, the heat, the vacant horizon."
A voice said: "It is no desert."

43

There came whisperings in the winds:
"Good-bye! Good-bye!"
Little voices called in the darkness:
"Good-bye! Good-bye!"
Then I stretched forth my arms.
"No— No—"
There came whisperings in the wind:
"Good-bye! Good-bye!"
Little voices called in the darkness:
"Good-bye! Good-bye!"

44

I was in the darkness;
I could not see my words
Nor the wishes of my heart.
Then suddenly there was a great light—

"Let me into the darkness again."

45

Tradition, thou art for suckling children,
Thou art the enlivening milk for babes;
But no meat for men is in thee.
Then—
But, alas, we all are babes.

46

Many red devils ran from my heart
And out upon the page.
They were so tiny
The pen could mash them.
And many struggled in the ink.
It was strange
To write in this red muck
Of things from my heart.

47

"Think as I think," said a man,
"Or you are abominably wicked;
You are a toad."

And after I had thought of it,
I said: "I will, then, be a toad."

48

Once there was a man,—
Oh, so wise!
In all drink
He detected the bitter,
And in all touch
He found the sting.
At last he cried thus:
"There is nothing,—
No life,
No joy,
No pain,—
There is nothing save opinion,
And opinion be damned."

49

I stood musing in a black world,
Not knowing where to direct my feet.
And I saw the quick stream of men
Pouring ceaselessly,
Filled with eager faces,
A torrent of desire.
I called to them:
"Where do you go? What do you see?"
A thousand voices called to me.
A thousand fingers pointed.
"Look! Look! There!"

I know not of it.
But, lo! in the far sky shone a radiance
Ineffable, divine,—
A vision painted upon a pall;
And sometimes it was,
And sometimes it was not.
I hesitated.
Then from the stream
Came roaring voices,
Impatient:
"Look! Look! There!"

So again I saw,
And leaped, unhesitant,
And struggled and fumed
With outspread clutching fingers.
The hard hills tore my flesh;
The ways bit my feet.
At last I looked again.
No radiance in the far sky,
Ineffable, divine,
No vision painted upon a pall;
And always my eyes ached for the light.
Then I cried in despair:
"I see nothing! Oh, where do I go?"
The torrent turned again its faces:
"Look! Look! There!"

And at the blindness of my spirit
They screamed:
"Fool! Fool! Fool!"

50

You say you are holy,
And that
Because I have not seen you sin.
Aye, but there are those
Who see you sin, my friend.

51

A man went before a strange god,—
The god of many men, sadly wise.
And the deity thundered loudly,
Fat with rage, and puffing:
"Kneel, mortal, and cringe
And grovel and do homage
To my particularly sublime majesty."

The man fled.

Then the man went to another god,—
The god of his inner thoughts.
And this one looked at him
With soft eyes
Lit with infinite comprehension,
And said: "My poor child!"

52

Why do you strive for greatness, fool?
Go pluck a bough and wear it.
It is as sufficing.

My Lord, there are certain barbarians
Who tilt their noses
As if the stars were flowers,
And thy servant is lost among their shoe-buckles.
Fain would I have mine eyes even with their eyes.

Fool, go pluck a bough and wear it.

53

I

Blustering god,
Stamping across the sky
With loud swagger,
I fear you not.
No, though from your highest heaven
You plunge your spear at my heart,
I fear you not.
No, not if the blow
Is as the lightning blasting a tree,
I fear you not, puffing braggart.

II

If thou can see into my heart
That I fear thee not,
Thou wilt see why I fear thee not,
And why it is right.
So threaten not, thou, with thy bloody spears,
Else thy sublime ears shall hear curses.

III

Withal, there is one whom I fear;
I fear to see grief upon that face.
Perchance, friend, he is not your god;
If so, spit upon him.
By it you will do no profanity.
But I—
Ah, sooner would I die
Than see tears in those eyes of my soul.

54

"It was wrong to do this," said the angel.
"You should live like a flower,
Holding malice like a puppy,
Waging war like a lambkin."

"Not so," quoth the man
Who had no fear of spirits;
"It is only wrong for angels
Who can live like the flowers,
Holding malice like the puppies,
Waging war like the lambkins."

55

A man toiled on a burning road,
Never resting.
Once he saw a fat, stupid ass
Grinning at him from a green place.
The man cried out in rage:
"Ah! do not deride me, fool!
I know you—
All day stuffing your belly,
Burying your heart
In grass and tender sprouts:
It will not suffice you."
But the ass only grinned at him from the green place.

56

A man feared that he might find an assassin;
Another that he might find a victim.
One was more wise than the other.

57

With eye and with gesture
You say you are holy.
I say you lie;
For I did see you
Draw away your coats
From the sin upon the hands
Of a little child.
Liar!

58

The sage lectured brilliantly.
Before him, two images:
"Now this one is a devil,
And this one is me."
He turned away.
Then a cunning pupil
Changed the positions.
Turned the sage again:
"Now this one is a devil,
And this one is me."
The pupils sat, all grinning,
And rejoiced in the game.
But the sage was a sage.

59

Walking in the sky,
A man in strange black garb
Encountered a radiant form.
Then his steps were eager;
Bowed he devoutly.
"My Lord," said he.
But the spirit knew him not.

60

Upon the road of my life,
Passed me many fair creatures,
Clothed all in white, and radiant.
To one, finally, I made speech:
"Who art thou?"
But she, like the others,
Kept cowled her face,
And answered in haste, anxiously:
"I am Good Deed, forsooth;
You have often seen me."
"Not uncowled," I made reply.
And with rash and strong hand,
Though she resisted,
I drew away the veil
And gazed at the features of Vanity.
She, shamefaced, went on;
And after I had mused a time,
I said of myself:
"Fool!"

61

I

There was a man and a woman
Who sinned.
Then did the man heap the punishment
All upon the head of her,
And went away gayly.

II

There was a man and a woman
Who sinned.
And the man stood with her.
As upon her head, so upon his,
Fell blow and blow,
And all people screaming: "Fool!"
He was a brave heart.

III

He was a brave heart.
Would you speak with him, friend?
Well, he is dead,
And there went your opportunity.
Let it be your grief
That he is dead
And your opportunity gone;
For, in that, you were a coward.

62

There was a man who lived a life of fire.
Even upon the fabric of time,
Where purple becomes orange
And orange purple,
This life glowed,
A dire red stain, indelible;
Yet when he was dead,
He saw that he had not lived.

63

There was a great cathedral.
To solemn songs,
A white procession
Moved toward the altar.
The chief man there
Was erect, and bore himself proudly.
Yet some could see him cringe,
As in a place of danger,
Throwing frightened glances into the air,
A-start at threatening faces of the past.

64 Friend, your white beard sweeps the ground.
Why do you stand, expectant?
Do you hope to see it
In one of your withered days?
With your old eyes
Do you hope to see
The triumphal march of justice?
Do not wait, friend!
Take your white beard
And your old eyes
To more tender lands.

65

Once, I knew a fine song,
—It is true, believe me,—
It was all of birds,
And I held them in a basket;
When I opened the wicket,
Heavens! they all flew away.
I cried: "Come back, little thoughts!"
But they only laughed.
They flew on
Until they were as sand
Thrown between me and the sky.

66 If I should cast off this tattered coat,
And go free into the mighty sky;
If I should find nothing there
But a vast blue,
Echoless, ignorant,—
What then?

67

God lay dead in Heaven;
Angels sang the hymn of the end;
Purple winds went moaning,
Their wings drip-dripping
With blood
That fell upon the earth.
It, groaning thing,
Turned black and sank.
Then from the far caverns
Of dead sins
Came monsters, livid with desire.
They fought,
Wrangled over the world,
A morsel.
But of all sadness this was sad,—
A woman's arms tried to shield
The head of a sleeping man
From the jaws of the final beast.

68 A spirit sped
Through spaces of night;
And as he sped, he called:
"God! God!"
He went through valleys
Of black death-slime,
Ever calling:
"God! God!"
Their echoes
From crevice and cavern
Mocked him:
"God! God! God!"
Fleetly into the plains of space
He went, ever calling:
"God! God!"
Eventually, then, he screamed,
Mad in denial:
"Ah, there is no God!"
A swift hand,
A sword from the sky,
Smote him,
And he was dead.

Uncollected Poems

"LEGENDS"

69

I

A man builded a bugle for the storms to blow.
The focussed winds hurled him afar.
He said that the instrument was a failure.

70

II

When the suicide arrived at the sky, the people
there asked him: "Why?"
He replied: "Because no one admired me."

71

III

A man said: "Thou tree!"
The tree answered with the same scorn: "Thou man!
Thou art greater than I only in thy possibilities."

72

IV

A warrior stood upon a peak and defied the stars.
A little magpie, happening there, desired the
soldier's plume, and so plucked it.

73

V

The wind that waves the blossoms sang, sang, sang
from age to age.
The flowers were made curious by this joy.
"Oh, wind," they said, "why sing you at your
labour, while we, pink beneficiaries, sing
not, but idle, idle, idle from age to age?"

74 When a people reach the top of a hill
Then does God lean toward them,
Shortens tongues, lengthens arms.
A vision of their dead comes to the weak.
The moon shall not be too old
Before the new battalions rise
—Blue battalions—
The moon shall not be too old
When the children of change shall fall
Before the new battalions
—The blue battalions—

Mistakes and virtues will be trampled deep
A church and a thief shall fall together
A sword will come at the bidding of the eyeless,
The God-led, turning only to beckon.
Swinging a creed like a censer
At the head of the new battalions
—Blue battalions—
March the tools of nature's impulse
Men born of wrong, men born of right
Men of the new battalions
—The blue battalions—

The clang of swords is Thy wisdom
The wounded make gestures like Thy Son's
The feet of mad horses is one part,
—Aye, another is the hand of a mother on the brow of a son.
    Then swift as they charge through a shadow,
    The men of the new battalions
        —Blue battalions—
    God lead them high. God lead them far
    Lead them far, lead them high
    These new battalions
        —The blue battalions—

75 Rumbling, buzzing, turning, whirling Wheels,
Dizzy Wheels!
Wheels!

War Is Kind

76

Do not weep, maiden, for war is kind.
Because your lover threw wild hands toward the sky
And the affrighted steed ran on alone,
Do not weep.
War is kind.

> Hoarse, booming drums of the regiment,
> Little souls who thirst for fight,
> These men were born to drill and die.
> The unexplained glory flies above them,
> Great is the Battle-God, great, and his Kingdom—
> A field where a thousand corpses lie.

Do not weep, babe, for war is kind.
Because your father tumbled in the yellow trenches,
Raged at his breast, gulped and died,
Do not weep.
War is kind.

> Swift blazing flag of the regiment,
> Eagle with crest of red and gold,
> These men were born to drill and die.
> Point for them the virtue of slaughter,
> Make plain to them the excellence of killing
> And a field where a thousand corpses lie.

Mother whose heart hung humble as a button
On the bright splendid shroud of your son,
Do not weep.
War is kind.

77

"What says the sea, little shell?
What says the sea?
Long has our brother been silent to us,
Kept his message for the ships,
Awkward ships, stupid ships."

"The sea bids you mourn, oh, pines,
Sing low in the moonlight.
He sends tale of the land of doom,
Of place where endless falls
A rain of women's tears,
And men in grey robes—
Men in grey robes—
Chant the unknown pain."

"What says the sea, little shell?
What says the sea?
Long has our brother been silent to us,
Kept his message for the ships,
Puny ships, silly ships."

"The sea bids you teach, oh, pines,
Sing low in the moonlight.
Teach the gold of patience,
Cry gospel of gentle hands,
Cry a brotherhood of hearts.
The sea bids you teach, oh, pines."

"And where is the reward, little shell?
What says the sea?
Long has our brother been silent to us,
Kept his message for the ships,
Puny ships, silly ships."

"No word says the sea, oh, pines,
No word says the sea.
Long will your brother be silent to you,
Keep his message for the ships,
Oh, puny pines, silly pines."

78

To the maiden
The sea was blue meadow
Alive with little froth-people
Singing.

To the sailor, wrecked,
The sea was dead grey walls
Superlative in vacancy
Upon which nevertheless at fateful time
Was written
The grim hatred of nature.

79 A little ink more or less!
It surely can't matter?
Even the sky and the opulent sea,
The plains and the hills, aloof,
Hear the uproar of all these books.
But it is only a little ink more or less.

What?
You define me God with these trinkets?
Can my misery meal on an ordered walking
Of surpliced numbskulls?
And a fanfare of lights?
Or even upon the measured pulpitings
Of the familiar false and true?
Is this God?
Where, then, is hell?
Show me some bastard mushroom
Sprung from a pollution of blood.
It is better.

Where is God?

80

"Have you ever made a just man?"
"Oh, I have made three," answered God,
"But two of them are dead
And the third—
Listen! Listen!
And you will hear the third of his defeat."

81

I explain the silvered passing of a ship at night,
The sweep of each sad lost wave
The dwindling boom of the steel thing's striving
The little cry of a man to a man
A shadow falling across the greyer night
And the sinking of the small star.

Then the waste, the far waste of waters
And the soft lashing of black waves
For long and in loneliness.

Remember, thou, O ship of love
Thou leavest a far waste of waters
And the soft lashing of black waves
For long and in loneliness.

82

"I have heard the sunset song of the birches
A white melody in the silence
I have seen a quarrel of the pines.
At nightfall
The little grasses have rushed by me
With the wind men.
These things have I lived," quoth the maniac,
"Possessing only eyes and ears.
But, you—
You don green spectacles before you look at roses."

83

Fast rode the knight——
With spurs, hot and reeking
Ever waving an eager sword.
"To save my lady!"
Fast rode the knight
And leaped from saddle to war.
Men of steel flickered and gleamed
Like riot of silver lights
And the gold of the knight's good banner
Still waved on a castle wall.

* * * * * * * * * * * *

A horse
Blowing, staggering, bloody thing
Forgotten at foot of castle wall.
A horse
Dead at foot of castle wall.

84

Forth went the candid man
And spoke freely to the wind—
When he looked about him he was in a far strange
 country.

Forth went the candid man
And spoke freely to the stars—
Yellow light tore sight from his eyes.

"My good fool," said a learned bystander,
"Your operations are mad."

"You are too candid," cried the candid man
And when his stick left the head of the learned
 bystander
It was two sticks.

85 You tell me this is God?
I tell you this is a printed list,
A burning candle and an ass.

86 On the desert
A silence from the moon's deepest valley.
Fire rays fall athwart the robes
Of hooded men, squat and dumb.
Before them, a woman
Moves to the blowing of shrill whistles
And distant-thunder of drums
While slow things, sinuous, dull with terrible
color
Sleepily fondle her body
Or move at her will, swishing stealthily over the
sand.
The snakes whisper softly;
The whispering, whispering snakes
Dreaming and swaying and staring
But always whispering, softly whispering.
The wind streams from the lone reaches
Of Arabia, solemn with night,
And the wild fire makes shimmer of blood
Over the robes of the hooded men
Squat and dumb.
Bands of moving bronze, emerald, yellow,
Circle the throat and the arms of her
And over the sands serpents move warily
Slow, menacing and submissive,
Swinging to the whistles and drums,
The whispering, whispering snakes,
Dreaming and swaying and staring
But always whispering, softly whispering.
The dignity of the accursèd;
The glory of slavery, despair, death
Is in the dance of the whispering snakes.

87

A newspaper is a collection of half-injustices
Which, bawled by boys from mile to mile,
Spreads its curious opinion
To a million merciful and sneering men,
While families cuddle the joys of the fireside
When spurred by tale of dire lone agony.
A newspaper is a court
Where every one is kindly and unfairly tried
By a squalor of honest men.
A newspaper is a market
Where wisdom sells its freedom
And melons are crowned by the crowd.
A newspaper is a game
Where his error scores the player victory
While another's skill wins death.
A newspaper is a symbol;
It is fetless life's chronicle,
A collection of loud tales
Concentrating eternal stupidities,
That in remote ages lived unhaltered,
Roaming through a fenceless world.

88

The wayfarer
Perceiving the pathway to truth
Was struck with astonishment.
It was thickly grown with weeds.
"Ha," he said,
"I see that none has passed here
In a long time."
Later he saw that each weed
Was a singular knife.
"Well," he mumbled at last,
"Doubtless there are other roads."

89

A slant of sun on dull brown walls
A forgotten sky of bashful blue.
Toward God a mighty hymn
A song of collisions and cries
Rumbling wheels, hoof-beats, bells,
Welcomes, farewells, love-calls, final moans,
Voices of joy, idiocy, warning, despair,
The unknown appeals of brutes,
The chanting of flowers
The screams of cut trees,
The senseless babble of hens and wise men—
A cluttered incoherency that says at the stars:
"O, God, save us."

90

Once, a man, clambering to the house-tops,
Appealed to the heavens.
With strong voice he called to the deaf spheres;
A warrior's shout he raised to the suns.
Lo, at last, there was a dot on the clouds,
And—at last and at last—
—God—the sky was filled with armies.

91

There was a man with tongue of wood
Who essayed to sing,
And in truth it was lamentable
But there was one who heard
The clip-clapper of this tongue of wood
And knew what the man
Wished to sing,
And with that the singer was content.

92

The successful man has thrust himself
Through the water of the years,
Reeking wet with mistakes,
Bloody mistakes;
Slimed with victories over the lesser
A figure thankful on the shore of money.
Then, with the bones of fools
He buys silken banners
Limned with his triumphant face;
With the skins of wise men
He buys the trivial bows of all.
Flesh painted with marrow
Contributes a coverlet
A coverlet for his contented slumber,
In guiltless ignorance, in ignorant guilt
He delivers his secrets to the riven multitude.
"Thus I defended: Thus I wrought."
Complacent, smiling,
He stands heavily on the dead.
Erect on a pillar of skulls
He declaims his trampling of babes;
Smirking, fat, dripping,
He makes speech in guiltless ignorance,
Innocence.

93

In the night
Grey heavy clouds muffled the valleys
And the peaks looked toward God, alone.
"Oh, Master that movest the wind with a finger,
Humble, idle, futile peaks are we.
Grant that we may run swiftly across the world
To huddle in worship at Thy feet."

In the morning
A noise of men at work came the clear blue miles
And the little black cities were apparent.
"Oh, Master that knowest the meaning of rain-drops,
Humble, idle, futile peaks are we.
Give voice to us, we pray, O Lord,
That we may sing Thy goodness to the sun."

In the evening
The far valleys were sprinkled with tiny lights.
"Oh, Master,
Thou who knowest the value of kings and birds,
Thou hast made us humble, idle, futile peaks.
Thou only needest eternal patience;
We bow to Thy wisdom, O Lord—
Humble, idle, futile peaks."

In the night
Grey heavy clouds muffled the valleys
And the peaks looked toward God, alone.

94 The chatter of a death-demon from a tree-top.

Blood—blood and torn grass—
Had marked the rise of his agony—
This lone hunter.
The grey-green woods impassive
Had watched the threshing of his limbs.

A canoe with flashing paddle
A girl with soft searching eyes,
A call: "John!"

* * * * * * * * *

Come, arise, hunter!
Can you not hear?

The chatter of a death-demon from a tree-top.

95 The impact of a dollar upon the heart
Smiles warm red light
Sweeping from the hearth rosily upon the white table,
With the hanging cool velvet shadows
Moving softly upon the door.

The impact of a million dollars
Is a crash of flunkeys
And yawning emblems of Persia
Cheeked against oak, France and a sabre,
The outcry of old beauty
Whored by pimping merchants
To submission before wine and chatter.
Silly rich peasants stamp the carpets of men,
Dead men who dreamed fragrance and light
Into their woof, their lives;
The rug of an honest bear
Under the feet of a cryptic slave
Who speaks always of baubles
Forgetting place, multitude, work and state,
Champing and mouthing of hats
Making ratful squeak of hats,
Hats.

96

A man said to the universe:
"Sir, I exist!"
"However," replied the universe,
"The fact has not created in me
A sense of obligation."

97

When the prophet, a complacent fat man,
Arrived at the mountain-top
He cried: "Woe to my knowledge!
I intended to see good white lands
And bad black lands—
But the scene is grey."

98

There was a land where lived no violets.
A traveller at once demanded: "Why?"
The people told him:
"Once the violets of this place spoke thus:
'Until some woman freely gives her lover
To another woman
We will fight in bloody scuffle.' "
Sadly the people added:
"There are no violets here."

99 [See *33* in *The Black Riders and Other Lines.*]

100

Aye, workman, make me a dream
A dream for my love.
Cunningly weave sunlight,
Breezes and flowers.
Let it be of the cloth of meadows.
And—good workman—
And let there be a man walking thereon.

101 Each small gleam was a voice
—A lantern voice—
In little songs of carmine, violet, green, gold.
A chorus of colors came over the water;
The wondrous leaf shadow no longer wavered,
No pines crooned on the hills
The blue night was elsewhere a silence
When the chorus of colors came over the water,
Little songs of carmine, violet, green, gold.

Small glowing pebbles
Thrown on the dark plane of evening
Sing good ballads of God
And eternity, with soul's rest.
Little priests, little holy fathers
None can doubt the truth of your hymning
When the marvellous chorus comes over the water
Songs of carmine, violet, green, gold.

102

The trees in the garden rained flowers.
Children ran there joyously.
They gathered the flowers
Each to himself.
Now there were some
Who gathered great heaps—
—Having opportunity and skill—
Until, behold, only chance blossoms
Remained for the feeble.
Then a little spindling tutor
Ran importantly to the father, crying:
"Pray, come hither!
See this unjust thing in your garden!"
But when the father had surveyed,
He admonished the tutor:
"Not so, small sage!
This thing is just.
For, look you,
Are not they who possess the flowers
Stronger, bolder, shrewder
Than they who have none?
Why should the strong—
—The beautiful strong—
Why should they not have the flowers?"

Upon reflection, the tutor bowed to the ground.
"My Lord," he said,
"The stars are displaced
By this towering wisdom."

"INTRIGUE"

103 Thou art my love
And thou art the peace of sundown
When the blue shadows soothe
And the grasses and the leaves sleep
To the song of the little brooks
Woe is me.

Thou art my love
And thou art a storm
That breaks black in the sky
And, sweeping headlong,
Drenches and cowers each tree
And at the panting end
There is no sound
Save the melancholy cry of a single owl
Woe is me!

Thou art my love
And thou art a tinsel thing
And I in my play
Broke thee easily
And from the little fragments
Arose my long sorrow
Woe is me

Thou art my love
And thou art a weary violet
Drooping from sun-caresses.
Answering mine carelessly
Woe is me.

Thou art my love
And thou art the ashes of other men's love
And I bury my face in these ashes
And I love them
Woe is me

Thou art my love
And thou art the beard
On another man's face
Woe is me.

Thou art my love
And thou art a temple
And in this temple is an altar
And on this altar is my heart
Woe is me.

Thou art my love
And thou art a wretch.
Let these sacred love-lies choke thee
For I am come to where I know your lies as truth
And your truth as lies
Woe is me.

Thou art my love
And thou art a priestess
And in thy hand is a bloody dagger
And my doom comes to me surely
Woe is me.

Thou art my love
And thou art a skull with ruby eyes
And I love thee
Woe is me.

Thou art my love
And I doubt thee
And if peace came with thy murder
Then would I murder.
Woe is me.

Thou art my love
And thou art death
Aye, thou art death
Black and yet black
But I love thee
I love thee
Woe, welcome woe, to me.

104

Love forgive me if I wish you grief
For in your grief
You huddle to my breast
And for it
Would I pay the price of your grief

You walk among men
And all men do not surrender
And this I understand
That love reaches his hand
In mercy to me.

He had your picture in his room
A scurvy traitor picture
And he smiled
—Merely a fat complacence
Of men who know fine women—
And thus I divided with him
A part of my love

Fool, not to know that thy little shoe
Can make men weep!
—Some men weep.
I weep and I gnash
And I love the little shoe
The little, little shoe.

God give me medals
God give me loud honors
That I may strut before you, sweetheart
And be worthy of—
—The love I bear you.

Now let me crunch you
With full weight of affrighted love
I doubted you
—I doubted you—
And in this short doubting
My love grew like a genie
For my further undoing.

Beware of my friends
Be not in speech too civil
For in all courtesy
My weak heart sees spectres,
Mists of desires
Arising from the lips of my chosen
Be not civil.

The flower I gave thee once
Was incident to a stride
A detail of a gesture
But search those pale petals
And see engraven thereon
A record of my intention

105

Ah, God, the way your little finger moved
As you thrust a bare arm backward
And made play with your hair
And a comb a silly gilt comb
Ah, God—that I should suffer
Because of the way a little finger moved.

106

Once I saw thee idly rocking
—Idly rocking—
And chattering girlishly to other girls,
Bell-voiced, happy,
Careless with the stout heart of unscarred womanhood
And life to thee was all light melody.
I thought of the great storms of love as I know it
Torn, miserable and ashamed of my open sorrow,
I thought of the thunders that lived in my head
And I wish to be an ogre
And hale and haul my beloved to a castle
And there use the happy cruel one cruelly
And make her mourn with my mourning

107 Tell me why, behind thee,
I see always the shadow of another lover?
Is it real
Or is this the thrice-damned memory of a better
happiness?
Plague on him if he be dead
Plague on him if he be alive
A swinish numbskull
To intrude his shade
Always between me and my peace

108

And yet I have seen thee happy with me.
I am no fool
To poll stupidly into iron.
I have heard your quick breaths
And seen your arms writhe toward me;
At those times
—God help us—
I was impelled to be a grand knight
And swagger and snap my fingers,
And explain my mind finely.
Oh, lost sweetheart,
I would that I had not been a grand knight.
I said: "Sweetheart."
Thou said'st: "Sweetheart."
And we preserved an admirable mimicry
Without heeding the drip of the blood
From my heart.

109

I heard thee laugh,
And in this merriment
I defined the measure of my pain;
I knew that I was alone,
Alone with love,
Poor shivering love,
And he, little sprite,
Came to watch with me,
And at midnight
We were like two creatures by a dead camp-fire.

110

I wonder if sometimes in the dusk,
When the brave lights that gild thy evenings
Have not yet been touched with flame,
I wonder if sometimes in the dusk
Thou rememberest a time,
A time when thou loved me
And our love was to thee all?
Is the memory rubbish now?
An old gown
Worn in an age of other fashions?
Woe is me, oh, lost one,
For that love is now to me
A supernal dream,
White, white, white with many suns.

111

Love met me at noonday,
—Reckless imp,
To leave his shaded nights
And brave the glare,—
And I saw him then plainly
For a bungler,
A stupid, simpering, eyeless bungler,
Breaking the hearts of brave people
As the snivelling idiot-boy cracks his bowl,
And I cursed him,
Cursed him to and fro, back and forth,
Into all the silly mazes of his mind,
But in the end
He laughed and pointed to my breast,
Where a heart still beat for thee, beloved.

112

I have seen thy face aflame
For love of me,
Thy fair arms go mad,
Thy lips tremble and mutter and rave.
And–surely–
This should leave a man content?
Thou lovest not me now,
But thou didst love me,
And in loving me once
Thou gavest me an eternal privilege,
For I can think of thee.

Posthumously Published Poems

113

A man adrift on a slim spar
A horizon smaller than the rim of a bottle
Tented waves rearing lashy dark points
The near whine of froth in circles.
God is cold.

The incessant raise and swing of the sea
And growl after growl of crest
The sinkings, green, seething, endless
The upheaval half-completed.
God is cold.

The seas are in the hollow of The Hand;
Oceans may be turned to a spray
Raining down through the stars
Because of a gesture of pity toward a babe.
Oceans may become grey ashes,
Die with a long moan and a roar
Amid the tumult of the fishes
And the cries of the ships,
Because The Hand beckons the mice.

A horizon smaller than a doomed assassin's cap,
Inky, surging tumults
A reeling, drunken sky and no sky
A pale hand sliding from a polished spar.
God is cold.

The puff of a coat imprisoning air:
A face kissing the water-death
A weary slow sway of a lost hand
And the sea, the moving sea, the sea.
God is cold.

114 Chant you loud of punishments,
Of the twisting of the heart's poor strings
Of the crash of the lightning's fierce revenge.

Then sing I of the supple-souled men
And the strong strong gods
That shall meet in times hereafter
And the amaze of the gods
At the strength of the men.
—The strong, strong gods—
—And the supple-souled men—

115 A naked woman and a dead dwarf;
Wealth and indifference.
Poor dwarf!
Reigning with foolish kings
And dying mid bells and wine
Ending with a desperate comic palaver
While before thee and after thee
Endures the eternal clown—
—The eternal clown—
A naked woman.

116

Little birds of the night
Aye, they have much to tell
Perching there in rows
Blinking at me with their serious eyes
Recounting of flowers they have seen and loved
Of meadows and groves of the distance
And pale sands at the foot of the sea
And breezes that fly in the leaves
They are vast in experience
These little birds that come in the night

117

Unwind my riddle.
Cruel as hawks the hours fly;
Wounded men seldom come home to die;
The hard waves see an arm flung high;
Scorn hits strong because of a lie;
Yet there exists a mystic tie.
Unwind my riddle.

118 Ah, haggard purse, why ope thy mouth
Like a greedy urchin
I have nought wherewith to feed thee
Thy wan cheeks have ne'er been puffed
Thou knowest not the fill of pride
Why then gape at me
In fashion of a wronged one
Thou do smilest wanly
And reproachest me with thine empty stomach
Thou knowest I'd sell my steps to the grave
If t'were but honestie
Ha, leer not so,
Name me no names of wrongs committed with thee
No ghost can lay hand on thee and me
We've been too thin to do sin
What, liar? When thou was filled of gold, didst I riot?
And give thee no time to eat?
No, thou brown devil, thou art stuffed now with lies as
with wealth,
The one gone to let in the other.

119

One came from the skies
—They said—
And with a band he bound them
A man and a woman.
Now to the man
The band was gold
And to another, iron
And to the woman, iron.
But this second man,
He took his opinion and went away
But, by heavens,
He was none too wise.

120

A god came to a man
And said to him thus:
"I have an apple
It is a glorious apple
Aye, I swear by my ancestors
Of the eternities before this eternity
It is an apple that is from
The inner thoughts of heaven's greatest.

"And this I will hang here
And then I will adjust thee here
Thus—you may reach it.
And you must stifle your nostrils
And control your hands
And your eyes
And sit for sixty years
But,—leave be the apple."

The man answered in this wise:
"Oh, most interesting God
What folly is this?
Behold, thou hast moulded my desires
Even as thou hast moulded the apple.

"How, then?
Can I conquer my life
Which is thou?
My desires?
Look you, foolish god
If I thrust behind me
Sixty white years
I am a greater god than God
And, then, complacent splendor,
Thou wilt see that the golden angels
That sing pink hymns
Around thy throne-top
Will be lower than my feet."

121

There is a grey thing that lives in the tree-tops
None know the horror of its sight
Save those who meet death in the wilderness
But one is enabled to see
To see branches move at its passing
To hear at times the wail of black laughter
And to come often upon mystic places
Places where the thing has just been.

122 If you would seek a friend among men
Remember: they are crying their wares.
If you would ask of heaven of men
Remember: they are crying their wares.
If you seek the welfare of men
Remember: they are crying their wares.
If you would bestow a curse upon men
Remember: they are crying their wares.
Crying their wares
Crying their wares
If you seek the attention of men
Remember:
Help them or hinder them as they cry their wares.

123 A lad and a maid at a curve in the stream
And a shine of soft silken waters
Where the moon-beams fall through a hemlock's boughs
Oh, night dismal, night glorious.

A lad and a maid at the rail of a bridge
With two shadows adrift on the water
And the wind sings low in the grass on the shore.
Oh, night dismal, night glorious.

A lad and a maid in a canoe,
And a paddle making silver turmoil

124 A soldier, young in years, young in ambitions
Alive as no grey-beard is alive
Laid his heart and his hopes before duty
And went staunchly into the tempest of war.
There did the bitter red winds of battle
Swirl 'gainst his youth, beat upon his ambitions,
Drink his cool clear blood of manhood
Until at coming forth time
He was alive merely as the greybeard is alive.
And for this—
The nation rendered to him a flower
A little thing—a flower
Aye, but yet not so little
For this flower grew in the nation's heart
A wet, soft blossom
From tears of her who loved her son
Even when the black battle rages
Made his face the face of furious urchin,
And this she cherished
And finally laid it upon the breast of him.
A little thing—this flower?
No—it was the flower of duty
That inhales black smoke-clouds
And fastens its roots in bloody sod
And yet comes forth so fair, so fragrant—
Its birth is sunlight in grimest, darkest place.

125 A row of thick pillars
Consciously bracing for the weight
Of a vanished roof
The bronze light of sunset strikes through them,
And over a floor made for slow rites.
There is no sound of singing
But, aloft, a great and terrible bird
Is watching a cur, beaten and cut,
That crawls to the cool shadows of the pillars
To die.

126 Oh, a rare old wine ye brewed for me
Flagons of despair
A deep deep drink of this wine of life
Flagons of despair.

Dream of riot and blood and screams
The rolling white eyes of dying men
The terrible heedless courage of babes

127

There exists the eternal fact of conflict
And—next—a mere sense of locality.
Afterward we derive sustenance from the winds.
Afterward we grip upon this sense of locality.
Afterward, we become patriots.
The godly vice of patriotism makes us slaves,
And—let us surrender to this falsity
Let us be patriots

Then welcome us the practical men
Thrumming on a thousand drums
The practical men, God help us.
They cry aloud to be led to war
Ah—
They have been poltroons on a thousand fields
And the sacked sad city of New York is their record
Furious to face the Spaniard, these people, and crawling worms before their task
They name serfs and send charity in bulk to better men
They play at being free, these people of New York
Who are too well-dressed to protest against infamy

128

On the brown trail
We hear the grind of your carts
To our villages,
Laden with food
Laden with food
We know you are come to our help
But—
Why do you impress upon us
Your foriegn happiness?
We know it not.
(Hark!
Carts laden with food
Laden with food)
We weep because we dont understand
But your gifts form into a yoke
The food turns into a yoke
(Hark!
Carts laden with food
Laden with food)
It is our mission to vanish
Grateful because of full mouths
Destiny—Darkness
Time understands
And ye—ye bigoted men of a moment—
—Wait—
Await your turn.

129 All-feeling God, hear in the war-night
The rolling voices of a nation;
Through dusky billows of darkness
See the flash, the under-light, of bared swords—
—Whirling gleams like wee shells
Deep in the streams of the universe—
Bend and see a people, O, God,
A people rebuked, accursed,
By him of the many lungs
And by him of the bruised weary war-drum
(The chanting disintegrate and the two-faced eagle)
Bend and mark our steps, O, God.
Mark well, mark well, Father of the Never-Ending Circles
And if the path, the new path, lead awry
Then in the forest of the lost standards
Suffer us to grope and bleed apace
For the wisdom is Thine.
Bend and see a people, O, God,
A people applauded, acclaimed,
By him of the raw red shoulders
The manacle-marked, the thin victim
(He lies white amid the smoking cane)

[NO STANZA BREAK]

—And if the path, the new path, leads straight—
Then—O, God—then bare the great bronze arm;
Swing high the blaze of the chained stars
And let them look and heed
(The chanting disintegrate and the two-faced eagle)
For we go, we go in a lunge of a long blue corps
And—to Thee we commit our lifeless sons,
The convulsed and furious dead.
(They shall be white amid the smoking cane)
For, the seas shall not bar us;
The capped mountains shall not hold us back
We shall sweep and swarm through jungle and pool,
Then let the savage one bend his high chin
To see on his breast, the sullen glow of the death-medals
For we know and we say our gift.
His prize is death, deep doom.
(He shall be white amid the smoking cane)

130

A grey and boiling street
Alive with rickety noise.
Suddenly, a hearse,
Trailed by black carriages
Takes a deliberate way
Through this chasm of commerce;
And children look eagerly
To find the misery behind the shades.
Hired men, impatient, drive with a longing
To reach quickly the grave-side, the end of
solemnity.

Yes, let us have it over.
Drive, man, drive.
Flog your sleek-hided beasts,
Gallop—gallop—gallop.
Let us finish it quickly.

131 Bottles and bottles and bottles
In a merry den
And the wan smiles of women
Untruthing license and joy.
Countless lights
Making oblique and confusing multiplication
In mirrors
And the light returns again to the faces.

* * * * * * * * * * *

A cellar, and a death-pale child.
A woman
Ministering commonly, degradedly,
Without manners.
A murmur and a silence
Or silence and a murmur
And then a finished silence.
The moon beams practically upon the cheap bed.

An hour, with its million trinkets of joy or
pain,
Matters little in cellar or merry den
Since all is death.

132 intermingled,
There come in wild revelling strains
Black words, stinging
That murder flowers
The horror of profane speculation.

133

The patent of a lord
And the bangle of a bandit
Make argument
Which God solves
Only after lighting more candles.

134

Tell me not in joyous numbers
We can make our lives sublime
By—well, at least, not by
Dabbling much in rhyme.

135 My cross!

Your cross?
The real cross
Is made of pounds,
Dollars or francs.
Here I bear my palms for the silly nails
To teach the lack
—The great pain of lack—
Of coin.

Index of First Lines